Be Encouraged

FROM TRAUMA TO WHOLENESS

A WOMAN'S DEVOTIONAL JOURNAL

A 90-Day Journal

Michelle Hurtt, LPC, ACTRP

Disclaimer: This devotional journal is meant to encourage, motivate and inspire women survivors of trauma. It is *not* meant to be advice or to replace the advice of a licensed mental health professional. The writings are drawn from the view of the author and from the author's own life experiences and lessons learned. If you are a trauma survivor, it is highly recommended that you seek help from a mental health professional to assist and guide you through the recovery process. If reading through this devotional journal, which provides examples of abuse, becomes too much for you, STOP. Dealing with trauma should be at YOUR own pace and while under the care of a mental health professional. If at anytime you begin to experience suicidal thoughts, engage in self-injurious behaviors, thoughts of harming someone else, or are in any type of crisis and need immediate assistance immediately call 911. Other sources of help could be to go to or contact the hospital nearest to you, call the National Suicide Prevention Lifeline: 1-800-273-TALK (8255), or reach out to a mental health professional.

TO

_____

FROM

_____

DATE

_____

Dedication

This journal is dedicated to and in loving memory of my sister Joanie, who has loved me unconditionally, especially during the times I most needed to feel loved.

It is also dedicated to my God-sister, Sharond Dempsey, who has also shown unconditional love, who has had the courage to take her own journey to wholeness and consistently reminds me of who I am in Jesus Christ.

And to my Aunt, Ann Daye, whose conversations have caused me to self-reflect, who encouraged me to mend relationships and encouraged me week after week to complete this work.

And, to all the courageous women (and men, though few) who have trusted me enough to share their stories and who also had the courage to begin their journey towards wholeness. It has truly been a privilege and an honor to serve you. You will forever be in my heart and prayers. I hope, somehow, this devotional journal makes its way to you and that you continue to travel on your pathway to wholeness.

Finally, to all the Angels along the way who allowed the Lord to use them as a guide and support for me on my journey to wholeness to His glory!

Fly Butterfly, Fly

I crawl and I crawl, and I push myself to go faster,

Life seems to be a never-ending journey,

Full of tough turns and painful falls.

I'm screaming for help but who could hear a caterpillar

I'm weak, I'm weak because this journey has defeated me

I fall to sleep, and I sleep, and I sleep

Until a new day begun . . . a new me has arrived

I have wings and now I can fly

My days are brighter, and I SHINE, I SHINE, I SHINE . . .

And then I Fly

Fly butterfly, fly!

Sharond Dempsey

DAY 1

What is Wrong With Me?
"Then they cried out to the Lord in their trouble,
And He saved them out of their distresses."

Psalm 107:19

Have you been asked: "What's wrong with you?" That is not the question to ask. It should be "what happened to you?" Have you ever thought "What *is* wrong with me?" Stop and think about that. Why do you act the way you do, say the things you do, and respond out of proportion to a given situation only to feel guilty about it later? Do you know the answer to these questions? Acknowledging and being consciously aware that something is not right are the first steps towards change and healing.

Take a minute to think about your history and what happened to you in your past. Just briefly. Were you abandoned, neglected, physically or sexually abused in your childhood? Or were you raped as a teen or adult, or beaten by someone who professed to love you? This is trauma. Any of these traumatic events could be the reason you do what you do, react the way you do and say the things you do.

Because of the trauma I suffered as a child, I spent many days during my young adulthood sitting or lying in bed staring into space. Not living, just existing. I did not know what was wrong with me then and I surely did not know that I was feeling that way because of the sexual abuse I suffered as a child.

I cried out to the Lord, even then, and He preserved me. I asked that He show me Himself and He did just that through people, situations, and things He placed along my path which all helped me on my journey to healing.

Are you ready for a change to take place in you, in your life? God will help you and is waiting for you to ask. What will you pray and ask for that new beginning?

DAY 1

DAY 2

You Are Not "Crazy!"

"For God has not given us a spirit of fear, but of power and of love and of a sound mind."

2 Timothy 1:7

Have you felt that something is just not right with the way you act and the things you say? Do you overreact or respond in an angry manner that is out of proportion to a given situation? Does your mind wander for long periods of time in the middle of a conversation, or when watching T.V.? Do you experience nightmares or intrusive memories of horrific things you experienced in your past? If your answer is yes, you could be functioning in a traumatized state. These are trauma responses which are normal after a traumatic event and are an indication that you may need help to be able to recover from whatever it was you have experienced. This does not mean you are crazy but that you have some work to do to be able to heal and be made whole. With help you may be able to recover and regain control of your life. Reaching out for help is a sign of strength not weakness.

If you are an adult survivor of childhood sexual abuse, physical abuse, neglect, or have been raped, know that what happened to you is not normal but that the way you have responded to these horrific acts *is* normal. Often emotional responses are heightened, emotions become dysregulated or out of control, or emotional numbness occurs after experiencing a traumatic event.

There is no shame in reaching out and asking for help. We were created to help one another and, at times, we need to seek wise counsel to help us overcome the trials we experience in life. Proverbs 11:14 says *"Where there is no counsel, the people fall; But in the multitude of counselors there is safety."*

Will you reach out for help? What are some steps you will take towards wholeness?

DAY 2

DAY 3

Why Me?

"And we know that all things work together for good to those who love God, to those who are the called according to His purpose."

Romans 8:28

Do I wonder why God allowed horrific things to happen to me as a child who was at the mercy of the parents *He* entrusted me to? Of course I do, but I also know that I would not be alive today if it were not for Jesus Christ, my Savior. I believe the reason it was me was because He knew I would be strong enough to make it through. He knew His purpose for my life was to help others who endured similar traumatic experiences but struggle to understand that it is the trauma that is negatively impacting their mind, body, and spirit. So, for me, it's all working "together for good."

You may never know the complete answer to the question "why me" regarding the horrific things you have experienced. Speculation may remain. But maybe you are now able to help someone else who has had a similar experience but continues to struggle.

I am sure you have heard stories of individuals who have started businesses or foundations to advocate for and support survivors of childhood sexual abuse or domestic violence and to educate the masses about prevention. These people often have experienced the same fate or know someone close to them who has. What if what happened to you is because God knows you are strong enough to reach out and help others. Could this be the answer to your why?

Because Jesus chose me, I can now say I am healed. Since He did it for me, He can and will do it for you. He chose you; will you choose Him?

Can you now answer the question "why me?"

DAY 3

DAY 4

"Home is Where Your Story Begins"
*"...Every kingdom divided against itself is brought to desolation,
and every city or house divided against itself will not stand."*

Matthew 12:25

I saw these words written on a decorative plaque. It hangs in my home today to remind me of how far I have come and what I have overcome. This statement is true, "home *is* where your story begins," whether that story is good or bad. Home means different things to different people. Home may be where you lived with your parents as a child and where you grew up experiencing a happy childhood, or an unhappy childhood. It could be where you were raised apart from your biological family. As an adult it could be where you live with your intimate partner, your spouse, and your children. As Jesus says in Matthew 12:25, *"a house divided against itself will not stand."* This division could result in families falling apart, resulting in children growing up in dysfunctional homes feeling unsafe and forced to endure chaos and confusion.

Unfortunately, for some, home is where the abuse happened and the abusers are family members. Children are taught not to tell what is happening inside the home and family secrets are kept. Sometimes when family members commit acts that are damaging, instead of facing the wrong, admitting the wrong and seeking forgiveness, shame causes them to keep it hidden at any cost, even to the point of denial and humiliating, degrading, or rejecting the victim. I'm sure you've heard of victim blaming, it's like that, a horrible thing to experience.

During your childhood, what was home like for you? Where is home for you now? What can you do as an adult to ensure your home is a safe place for everyone, especially your children?

DAY 4

DAY 5

Forgiving is Not Forgetting
"And whenever you stand praying, if you have anything
against anyone, forgive him, that your Father in
heaven may also forgive you your trespasses."

Mark 11:25

Forgiveness is a sign of strength not weakness. Forgiveness can be freeing. It's part of the healing process. Forgiving others is more for you than it is for the person being forgiven. Forgiving that person who has caused you harm will free you of the bitterness, resentment, and anger you may have held tightly for far too long. Yet, forgiving is not forgetting.

A quote by Marianne Williamson says *"Unforgiveness is like drinking poison yourself and waiting for the other person to die."* Holding on to unforgiveness for long periods of time can be detrimental to a person's health and wellbeing. Forgiving someone does not mean that your relationship with that person must continue, and it does not mean that you must continue to keep yourself in harm's way or be in the presence of that person. You can express forgiveness directly to the person being forgiven but there can also be forgiveness in their absence. Forgiveness comes from the heart. You make mistakes, I make mistakes, we all make mistakes at some time in our lives, and we also do things we know are wrong. It is also important for us to forgive ourselves, which is just as important as forgiving others.

So, what do we do? Jesus said in Luke 23:34, *"Father, forgive them for they know not what they do."* Forgiving someone who has abused you or has stood by knowing the abuse was occurring and did nothing is a difficult thing to do. Yet, forgiveness can free you from the hurt and pain, from the bitterness, anger and resentment resulting from the wrong done to you.

Are there family members who you need to forgive? Who are they? Do you choose to forgive them? Is there anyone else you should forgive?

DAY 5

DAY 6

Trauma Does Not Define You

"For we are His workmanship, created in Christ Jesus for good works, which God prepared beforehand that we should walk in them."

Ephesians 2:10

It may be an enormous bump in the road meant to throw you off course, but trauma does not define you. It is something that happened to you, it is not who you are. You are a child of God. We were created to do good things for ourselves and for others. I hope you are willing to start your healing journey and get back on track to do what the Lord has planned for you to do.

If you are reading this devotional journal, most likely, you have survived something horrific or know someone who has. The first step towards healing from a traumatic experience is being aware and acknowledging that what happened to you has affected you emotionally, mentally and in some cases, physically to the point of interfering with your ability to effectively function in daily life. Traumatic experiences need to be resolved and you may need the help of a professional to process that trauma and for support and guidance.

Please do not allow your past to define you. I spent most of my adult life trying to *prove* that I am smarter than what the abusers and naysayers in my life tried to make me believe. I now know that I do not have to prove anything to anyone. I know who I am and whose I am. I hope the same for you. You and I only need to be the best human beings we can be. God knows us and has known us from our mothers' wombs. He knows what we've been through, and He knows our hearts.

You can heal and overcome that thing to do the *"good works"* that God has predestined you to do.

What are God's plans for you? What are your God-given gifts and talents?

DAY 6

DAY 7

Know the Signs
*"But take heed to yourselves, lest your hearts be weighed
down with carousing, drunkenness, and cares of this
life, and that Day come on you unexpectedly."*

Luke 21:34

Yes, horrific things have happened to us, sometimes it seems too much for us to bear. Studies have shown that there is a connection between traumatic experiences and substance abuse. When trauma is unresolved, some trauma survivors turn to drugs or alcohol or engage in other self-destructive behaviors such as cutting in an effort to escape the suffering from emotional pain, to cope or to drown out memories hoping to forget what has happened to them. These can be signs of trauma and negative ways of coping.

There are many other signs of unresolved trauma such as flashbacks, nightmares, depression, being constantly on guard and easily started, exaggerated emotional responses (responding out of proportion to a given situation) and mood swings, just to name a few, as well as trauma related body sensations. These things are telling your body and mind that you have not healed from what has happened to you.

Try educating yourself about trauma. Each person may respond differently to events that are perceived to be traumatic. Some may be resilient enough to show no signs of trauma when another may show many signs. These signs may not show up until many years later. A mental health professional can help you identify any signs you may be experiencing, determine if the signs are trauma related and how to overcome or cope with them.

Yes, what has happened to you is devastating, but life is short! Too short to allow what has happened to you consume you. Jesus knows what you have done to protect yourself. He knows those temptations. And, He has promised to help you. All you need do is ask.

What is it that you will ask Jesus to help you with today?

DAY 7

DAY 8

Gomer Did Not Know

"She will chase her lovers, But not overtake them; Yes, she will seek
them, but not find them. Then she will say, 'I will go and return
to my first husband, For then it was better for me than now.'"

Hosea 2:7

Gomer and Hosea's story is known to be about God's love for His people. Even when His people turned away from Him, He continued to love them. God commanded Hosea to love his wife, Gomer, and to go and find her after she left him for another man (Hosea 3:1). Not much is said about Gomer and her life before her relationship with Hosea. However, she was known as an adulterous and, from reading her story, she could have been a prostitute. Her promiscuity could have been a sign of sexual trauma occurring some time in her life. We do not know what happened to her but clearly, she was functioning in a traumatized state.

I have often wondered why Gomer engaged in risky sexual behavior. Was it a cry for help? We can only speculate. Although there are some survivors who avoid sexual relations altogether, statistics show that there is a high correlation between childhood sexual abuse and prostitution and an increased likelihood that survivors of childhood sexual abuse will engage in promiscuous behavior or prostitution. I recently read a book by Dr. Peter Levine that answered many questions about healing from sexual trauma that, for me, had remained unanswered. In his book *"Healing Trauma,"* he speaks about "the compulsion to repeat the actions that caused the problem [symptoms] in the first place," which can come about because of unresolved trauma. He gives "the prostitute or stripper with a history of childhood sexual trauma" as an example (p.19). Gomer did not know. Could this be you?

Is there anything happening within you (shown outwardly) that you do not understand? What is it? Will you seek help?

DAY 8

DAY 9

The Moment Things Changed

"Through the Lord's mercies we are not consumed,
because His compassions fail not."

Lamentations 3:22

You are living your life as normal. Then, something happens that changes your life forever and after you will never be the same. That's what I call a pivotal moment. It may have been a good thing, or it may have been traumatic. The good pivotal moments could be getting that well-paying first job, earning a degree, getting married, or having your first child. Tragic pivotal moments could be when you were abused or abandoned as a child, being hit the first time by a spouse, being raped, or the unexpected death of a close loved one. These tragic pivotal moments may never be forgotten.

Hopefully, despite it all, you will consider your survival a good thing. You were not consumed. You will have ups and downs because of your memories of that day as you make efforts to recover and become whole again. As I traveled my road to recovery, I often asked myself, when I thought of that tragic pivotal moment and the days and years of abuse that followed, "what was I begun for?" I didn't know the answer to that question until many years later. All I knew for sure was that God loved me and that *knowing* is what helped me make it through the days and years of abuse that followed.

It could be said the pivotal moment for Jesus was when He knew His life on earth would end on the cross.

God is all-knowing and He cares for you. Yes, He does! You may be thinking if He loves me then why . . .? We may never know the answer to so many of our why questions. But through it all we were *not consumed* and (I believe) survived for a reason.

What will be your prayer about your pivotal moment?

DAY 9

DAY 10

The Journey

"For I know the thoughts that I think toward you, says the Lord,
thoughts of peace and not of evil, to give you a future and a hope."

Jeremiah 29:11

Things happened to some of us as children that were beyond our control leaving us traumatized, wounded, and feeling desperately alone. Then later in life suppressed feelings of bitterness, resentment, and anger begin to surface. But, praise God, His mercies are brand new each morning (Lamentations 3:22-23).

Recovery from trauma is a journey. There is no quick fix, although you may be able to recover. It takes work, it takes commitment, it takes time. The journey will be long and hard and there will be ups and downs. You must find your own pathway to healing and go at your own pace.

There is a poem by Portia Nelson called *"There's a Hole in My Sidewalk,"* which talks about walking down a street where there is a hole in the sidewalk, repeatedly walking down that same street and falling into the hole even knowing that the hole is there. It reminds me of the so-called definition of insanity "doing the same thing over and over again and expecting a different result."

In a TED Talk writer Pico Iyer said, "It's only by stopping movement that you know where to go." It was after hearing this statement that I then knew what God meant when he said in Psalm 46:10 (KJV) *"Be still and know that I am God."* Because it is in the stillness of the day and night that we can hear His Spirit within us telling us what we need to know and what we should do. When you truly know what God's purpose is for your life and walk in it, therein lies your happiness and joy. There will be Angels along the way who God has sent your way to help you.

Will you be still so that you can hear the way you should go? Write it here.

DAY 10

DAY 11

Where is Your Safe Place?

"He shall cover you with His feathers,
And under His wings you shall take refuge;
His truth shall be your shield and buckler."

Psalm 91:4

Abuse comes in many forms. It can be physical, sexual, verbal, emotional, mental, and financial. Before healing can begin you must be in a safe place. Living in a place where there is ongoing domestic violence or where your children are being abused is not a safe place.

Places where you find refuge from the outside world and away from those who have caused or are causing you harm may be places of safety. A place where you can retreat and be at peace. Your safe place could be with a trusted family member or close friend. You may feel safe in the arms of a loving and caring partner. God promises to cover you with His feathers and under His wings for protection. He promises He will provide all your needs in Philippians 4:19. There are many more scriptures regarding protection for you to explore.

If you are currently in a domestically violent situation, check the Resources at the end of this devotional journal for help. One resource listed is the National Domestic Violence Hotline (1-800-799-SAFE (7233)), a hotline that is available 7 days a week, 24 hours a day and provides crisis intervention, safety planning, referrals, and resources, including safe havens for victims of domestic violence. ***Should you decide to leave a violent partner, have a safety plan in place which should include a safe place for you to go.*** The Office on Women's Health website at www.womenshealth.gov has a wealth of information about relationships and safety. The National Domestic Violence Hotline website at www.hotline.org provides a guide for creating a safety plan. At www.domesticshelters.org you can find help for locating shelters nationwide and in Canada and a safety planning worksheet which includes collecting evidence of domestic violence.

Where is your safe place?

DAY 11

DAY 12

Awareness, the First Step Towards Change
"Take heed to yourself and to the doctrine.
Continue in them, for in doing this you will save
both yourself and those who hear you."

1 Timothy 4:16

Awareness is key and the first step towards change. If you are unaware or ignore that something is wrong with you, nothing will be done to correct it. Once you become aware that something *is* wrong, acknowledging the fact that help may be needed to recover from what has happened to you is vital, otherwise nothing will change. It is important to act.

A next step could be to educate yourself about what could be causing you to say what you say and react the way you do that is harmful to yourself and others. Take note of others' reactions to what you say and do to pick up on potential signs that these reactions could be trauma responses.

There are good things and bad things about us all. Some of these things are because of the choices we make. Getting to know your true self, the things you can change and the things you cannot change, like is said in the Serenity Prayer, is important. You can learn new ways of coping when you are aware of the need. For in so doing you could save yourself and others from harm. It takes work, time, and patience to discover and address unresolved trauma and to eventually discover your true self.

List at least 3 things you can do to begin discovering your true self.

DAY 12

DAY 13

Identify Your Inner Strength
"But those who wait on the Lord shall renew their strength;
they shall mount up with wings like eagles, they shall run
and not be weary, they shall walk and not faint.

Isaiah 40:31

Trauma can weaken us emotionally, mentally and physically, depending upon the type of trauma. The Lord promises to renew our strength so we can move forward and fulfill His purpose for our life. We can become emotionally and mentally strong, and sometimes physically strong even after a traumatic event. We can exercise to become physically strong and meditate on the Word to become emotionally and mentally strong, along with prayer.

Inner strength is important to the healing process. It is being emotionally strong, mentally strong, persevering, being able to overcome obstacles and not giving up. It is being resilient, being able to bounce back and being able to speak up for yourself. When we apply for a job the questions "what are your strengths," and "what are your weaknesses" are often asked. Do you know the answers to these questions? Having experienced a traumatic event makes it even more important to know your strengths and your weaknesses.

Knowing and using your inner strengths may help you to overcome what may have been holding you back until now. The importance of knowing your weaknesses is so that you know in what areas you need help for your journey ahead. Knowing your weaknesses and strengths and what you are good at will help with identifying your life purpose.

What are your weaknesses? What are your strengths? What can you do to demonstrate inner strength? Identify a Bible verse that you can recite from memory when you need to show your inner strength.

DAY 13

DAY 14

Know What Triggers You

"Remember my affliction and roaming, The wormwood and the gall. My soul still remembers and sinks within me."

Lamentations 3:19-20

When people see you suffering, they may say "just get over it," or "just let it go." They often have good intentions when they say these things, but they do not understand that there are invisible scars that linger after a traumatic event. You can't get over it or let it go because what happened haunts you through nightmares, flashbacks and as you go about your daily life when memories of your suffering are triggered.

Triggers can be people, places, situations, things that cause flashbacks of traumatic events, dissociation, panic attacks, intense anger sometimes to the point of rage, and nightmares. Using the 5 senses: what you see, what you hear, what you smell, what you touch, what you taste can be helpful in identifying what triggers you. It's important to your recovery to learn what your triggers are.

By knowing what your triggers are you then know the people, places, situations, and things you should avoid at least until you learn how to effectively respond when triggered. A trained trauma therapist can help you with this.

Do you know what your triggers are?

What are some ways you can respond differently when you are triggered?

DAY 14

DAY 15

Challenge Those Negative Thoughts

"Finally, brethren, whatever things are true, whatever things are noble, whatever things are just, whatever things are pure, whatever things are lovely, whatever things are of good report, if there is any virtue and if there is anything praiseworthy--meditate on these things."

Philippians 4:8

For whatever reason, our minds tend to automatically lean towards the negative. Does that happen to you? Do you experience racing thoughts, negative thoughts that play in your mind over and over again? For peace of mind, it is important to learn how to control your thoughts and not allow your thoughts to control you. This scripture verse directs our thoughts to the positive.

There is a commonly used therapeutic treatment called cognitive-behavioral therapy through which people can be taught how to identify, challenge, and replace automatic inaccurate, unhealthy, or negative thoughts with the positive. These unhealthy thoughts can cause negative feelings which in turn can cause negative actions. Thus, the importance of addressing these thoughts.

Part of the healing process is to consistently practice challenging and replacing recurring unhealthy or negative thoughts with realistic, healthy, or helpful thoughts. Keep in mind that healthy, encouraging thoughts can help you to feel upbeat resulting in you responding in a more positive way. As in the scripture verse above, God reminds us to meditate on good things.

Name a few negative recurring thoughts that you could or should challenge. What could be healthy replacement thoughts?

DAY 15

DAY 16

Calm Instead of Panic

*"Be anxious for nothing, but in everything by prayer and
supplication, with thanksgiving, let your requests be made known
to God; and the peace of God, which surpasses all understanding,
will guard your hearts and minds through Christ Jesus."*

Philippians 4:6-7

There are many things that cause us to panic. Life has its ups and downs, and things happen unexpectedly. Some things that cause us to panic may be trauma related, some not. Panic and fear are two things for which triggers can be identified.

Think of people, places, situations, and things that could possibly cause you to panic and become fearful. When panic and fear are triggered, do you respond out of proportion to a given situation? That's what having experienced a traumatic event can do. Thinking ahead to what might be encountered throughout your day and preparing yourself for how you might respond ahead of time could help you respond in a more controlled manner. Also, when you take the time to think about what you might encounter could be the time to pray for guidance about whatever that might be and how to respond.

Pray during bad times and good. Pray for strength, courage, perseverance, blessings, and peace. Pray about the things you are grateful for despite what you have been through. Pray "in everything." God promises to give you peace and to guard your heart and mind – therein lies the calm. These are just a few of His many promises that are revealed in His Word.

What do you have planned to do tomorrow?

Will you encounter any possible triggers for panic or fear? If so, how will you respond?

What scripture will you read to achieve peace and calm as you face your day?

DAY 16

DAY 17

Self -Control
"Whoever has no rule over his own spirit is like
a city broken down, without walls."

Proverbs 25:28

Are you able to control your emotions? Are you able to control your words? Are you able to control your actions, or your manner of being? If not, you could be feeling a sense of brokenness and without the ability to set boundaries. In this condition a person is left open to ongoing abuse, hurt and pain. If you are a trauma survivor, this may sound familiar to you. But it does not have to remain this way.

There are times when we lose our temper and say things we wish we hadn't said or done things we should apologize for. But do you do these things so often it has become a habit, or do you learn from these behaviors and make better choices?

Emotion dysregulation is a person's inability to regulate their own emotions. For some it can be a struggle to maintain self-control and it could be one of the aftereffects of trauma. There is hope and self-control can be learned.

Being aware that something needs to change is key. There is no need to go it alone. Look at the list of resources at the end of this devotional journal. Help is waiting for you there.

What will you do the next time someone triggers you to anger? What will you say?

Will you reach out for help today?

DAY 17

DAY 18

Remember to Breathe

"Thus saith the Lord God unto these bones; Behold, I will
cause breath to enter into you, and ye shall live."

Ezekiel 37:5 (KJV)

There is a song called *"Breathe"* by Jonny Diaz. He speaks in this song about how hectic life can be and our needing to take the time to stop and consciously take a deep breath! He also speaks of the need to seek the peace of God to help us through the trials and tribulations we may be experiencing. Give yourself time to sort things out and decide what to do next.

When you are feeling overwhelmed, stop and simply breathe. There are a few widely known breathing techniques that can be used to help you do just that. It works for some but not for others. It's worth trying a few to see if any of them works for you.

One such technique is called "controlled breathing" which is to take a deep breath through your nose, hold for a few seconds and then slowly exhale through your mouth, being aware of your breathing until you begin to feel calm and relaxed.

Jesus says we should "learn" from Him and we will "find rest for [our] souls" (Matthew 11:29).

Will you search for a breathing technique that works for you? Which breathing technique will you try?

What prayer will you pray as a reminder to stop and simply breathe when you begin to feel overwhelmed?

DAY 18

DAY 19

Be Angry Without Sinning
"He who is slow to wrath has great understanding,
But he who is impulsive exalts folly."

Proverbs 14:29

Often after trauma survivors remain in defense mode. You may react out of proportion to a given situation because you are stuck in defense mode. That could be responding in an angry outburst even to the point of rage. It is okay to become angry, we all do, but it is how we respond when angered that makes a difference. It would be helpful to try to stop and think before reacting, although this may be hard to do. However, it is important to learn how to control our impulses so that we can respond to any given situation in an appropriate manner.

God says we are to be slow to anger. During my teen years I was angry and afraid but consciously did not know why. I did not understand that the abuse I was forced to endure was impacting me in this way. As an adult and looking back I realize I was angry and afraid because the adults around me did not take the time to figure out what was wrong with me, nor did they ask. There were some who knew what was happening but failed to act which also caused me to remain angry during those years. Even then I knew God was with me because of the kindness and love shown towards me from those outside of the home. That gave me hope and strengthened my belief that one day I would be free. You too can be made free.

There will be people who provoke you to anger, especially those who know how to push your buttons. When provoked maybe count to 10 to see if that works for you, or simply walk away. Figure out what works for you to control your anger.

Do you sometimes respond in anger out of proportion to a given situation? Do you understand why?

What can you do instead? What are some healthy ways to respond when you become angry?

DAY 19

DAY 20

Be Mindful of What you Say

"Let no corrupt word proceed out of your mouth, but what is good for necessary edification, that it may impart grace to the hearers."

Ephesians 4:29

Just as God's Word is powerful, the words we speak are powerful. Our words can hurt, cause sadness and pain and express hate. Functioning in a traumatized state people can use harmful words out of fear and as a defense mechanism to keep people at a distance.

Fortunately, words can also uplift, encourage, motivate, inspire, and express love. Proverbs 16:24 says *"Pleasant words are like a honeycomb, sweetness to the soul and health to the bones."* It doesn't take much effort to speak a kind word.

We don't know what a person has been through either in their past or today, so a kind word will go a long way. Sometimes simply saying "hi," with a smile may help a lonely person feel not so alone because you acknowledge that you see her or him. Why not try it today.

Proverbs 18:21 says, in part, *"death and life are in the power of the tongue."* To me this means words that speak death are those words that hurt, demean, and degrade a person and make them feel less than. Words that speak life are those words that are an expression of love, caring, kindness, uplifting and express compassion. Remember it can be as little as a "hi" and a smile that can make a person's day. Try it and see for yourself that it works!

What are some words you can say to others throughout your day today to lift someone's spirit, encourage and inspire?

What are some words you can say to motivate and encourage yourself?

DAY 20

DAY 21

Depression – The Slow Lullaby

"Anxiety in the heart of man causes depression,
but a good word makes it glad."

Proverbs 12:25

Have you ever been depressed? What was it like for you? Were you able to overcome it? Depression is a secondary sign of trauma. It is characterized by sadness, loneliness, hopelessness, helplessness, lack of interest in things once enjoyed, withdrawing from others. Generally, it does not come upon us all at once. It's gradual, creeps up on us, cuddles us like a slow lullaby but unlike a baby who makes every effort to resist falling asleep, there often is no resistance when falling into a state of depression.

Depression can be like fog descending upon the earth, quiet, slow moving, captivating yet unassuming. Those who are in its grasp may attempt to escape the feeling by sleeping hour after hour, night into day, day into night. Often it comes upon us before we realize what is happening.

Just as is described in the scripture above, *"a good word makes [a heart] glad."* If you know someone who may be depressed try sharing a kind word, although this may not be enough, it could help in some instances. If you know someone who is experiencing deep depression, encourage them to get help. If he or she is expressing a desire to harm themselves, please take it seriously. The National Suicide Prevention Lifeline number is 1-800-273-TALK (8255). This Lifeline provides 24/7, free and confidential support for people in distress; prevention and crisis resources for you or loved ones. The website for the National Suicide Presentation Lifeline is www.suicidepreventionlifeline.org. The National Suicide Prevention Lifeline number in Spanish (numero en Español) is 1-888-628-9454.

Do you know of someone who may be in need of help or support? If so, please share these numbers. What are you willing to do to support and help them or yourself if you are in need?

DAY 21

DAY 22

He Hears Your Heart's Cry
"The righteous cry out, and the Lord hears, And
delivers them out of all their troubles."

Psalm 34:17

There are tears of joy and tears of mourning and sorrow. At times people experience crying spells when depressed and when thinking about their horrific past. It's normal and it's okay to cry. There is healing in your tears and no shame in it. Crying is part of the healing process. John 11:35 says *"Jesus wept."* So, who are we to be ashamed to cry when we know that Jesus Himself cried?

Psalm 30:5 says *". . . weeping may endure for a night, but joy comes in the morning."* What does this mean? That joy will eventually come? It will, *eventually*.

To God, one day is like a 1,000 years and a 1,000 years like one day (2 Peter 3:8). Wait patiently, He hears your cry!

Have you ever felt a sense of peace after a good, long cry? I have and have felt a wave of peace and calm after. It is good to sit in our emotions from time to time.

As you wait and hope for that joy that the Lord promises to come – a day, a night, a week, a month, a year - focus on your blessings for there is joy in them. Count what you are grateful for. Be thankful.

What *are* you grateful for? Make a list.

DAY 22

DAY 23

Grieve the Loss

"Blessed are those who mourn; for they shall be comforted."

Matthew 5:4

There are many things that can make us sad, but we push through it. Don't we? Mourning, grieving is part of the healing process after trauma. Grieving the losses resulting from trauma is often overlooked when we think of healing from trauma. But think about it. After trauma there can be the loss of relationships, the loss of a childhood, the loss of innocence after childhood sexual abuse. There can be the loss of a sense of safety and the loss of the willingness to trust especially after sexual trauma and domestic violence.

It is important to grieve these losses to be able to move forward. Remember, crying is okay as you go through the grieving process and can have a cleansing affect. Finding a way to comfort yourself or being with someone who is comforting and who you can trust when memories arise can help. Grieving is important for recovery.

Because of trauma-related losses, new relationships need to be formed or old relationships renewed (not all). A sense of safety must be restored and the ability to trust again. Counseling can help in this regard.

Was it a loss of your childhood that you need to grieve?

Was it the loss of relationships?

Was it a loss of innocence?

Identify your losses and process these losses with a counselor or with someone you do trust.

DAY 23

DAY 24

What Do You Need?

*"And my God shall supply all your need according
to His riches in glory by Christ Jesus."*

Philippians 4:19

Have you heard of Maslow's Hierarchy of Needs? It is well known to be a model of different levels of human needs and includes needs that are important for human survival such as food, water, shelter and clothing; the need for safety, a sense of feeling safe and secure; the need to be loved and a sense of belonging and feeling connected; self-esteem which is a sense of self-worth and the need to be respected; and personal growth and working towards being the best one can be. It's easy to find a chart of these needs online. Take a look for deeper insight when you have a minute.

Note that love is listed as a human need. God says, *"the greatest of these is love"* (1 Corinthians 13:13) and *"God is love"* (1 John 4:8 and 1 John 4:16). We all need to be loved and should also give love.

You may not know how to love because of the damage done from the abuse, but you can learn. You may not know what it is like to feel loved, but know God loves you! You can ask Him to show His love towards you. Ask Him to help you *feel* His love. He will. Look for the signs. He may show it through a person you know or even through the act of a stranger, a boss or co-worker. You'll know it when you feel it.

God promises to provide *"all your need according to **His riches**"* not yours!

Do you know the needs that have gone unmet for you?

Right now, what would you say you need? How will you fulfill those needs?

DAY 24

DAY 25

You Can Learn to Trust Again

"Trust in the Lord with all your heart, And lean not on
your own understanding; In all your ways acknowledge
Him, And He shall direct your paths."

Proverbs 3:5-6

Often with trauma, there is a betrayal of trust. If this occurs during childhood, especially by someone who was supposed to care for you, love you and meet your needs, there is no foundation upon which to build trusting relationships as you grow into adulthood. You may not even trust people in general. If you are unable to trust because of what happened to you, I hope that you can at least trust in God and remain hopeful in Him. Trust is not freely given, especially after trauma, it must be earned. Who should you trust? Who can you trust? It has been said we should trust until people prove themselves to be untrustworthy. What are your thoughts about that?

It is extremely difficult if not impossible to go through life alone. God created us to help one another, and the Bible says that it is not good for us to be alone (Genesis 2:18). Studies have shown that living alone can negatively impact longevity which is also proof that we need one another.

After trauma knowing who to trust can be very difficult and you may experience self-doubt. Learn to trust your instincts while at the same time look for red flags at the beginning of new relationships. For intimate relationships take it slow and ask someone you *do* trust if they have noticed anything that does not seem right about the person you are interested in having a relationship. Then, stay in prayer about every relationship.

Identify at least one person (more if you can) you can confide in and why.

DAY 25

DAY 26

Are you Afraid?

*"Fear not, for I am with you; Be not dismayed, for I am
your God. I will strengthen you, Yes, I will help you, I
will uphold you with My righteous right hand."*

Isaiah 41:10

This is one of my favorite scriptures. I recited it out loud and quietly within
when abandoned by a spouse while living in a big city, when riding and waiting
for a bus, when fearing (as a single mother) that I would not be able to pay rent,
and in so many other instances throughout my life. Fear haunted me. For years I
meditated on and recited this verse and it worked. It gave me courage, hope and
strength and I often felt God's presence as I moved through these trying times.

It has been said that fear is the opposite of faith. You may have heard that
statement at some time during your life. I believe it to be true. If I am *afraid* that a
sturdy chair will break when I sit on it, most likely I will not sit on it even though
its breaking is highly unlikely. If I believe that chair will remain sturdy and strong,
I am more likely to sit on it because I believe - *have faith* - it will not break. Faith
in God is the confidence, trust and belief that He will do what He says He will do.

If you believe God does not hear you when you pray, you are most likely not
going to pray. If you believe, have faith, that He hears you, you are most likely to
pray. He says He will help us and strengthen us. Hold strong to your faith.

When might this scripture help you? What are you afraid of?

Identify at least 3 fears. If you are ready, safely – in prayer - confront at least
one of those identified fears today. You don't have to do it alone.

What was the outcome? Hopefully it was a success!! Fear not!

DAY 26

DAY 27

Heal from Emotional Pain

"He heals the brokenhearted and binds up their wounds."

Psalm 147:3

Emotional abuse can result in traumatic wounding. One of those being emotional pain. Of course, there are other causes for emotional pain like the losses mentioned previously. The suffering from emotional abuse sometimes is not acknowledged and therefore may go untreated. Emotional pain is one of those lingering signs a trauma survivor often endures, and which can lead to self-harm such as cutting. Cutting is often done to escape emotional pain. This needs to be acknowledged and addressed as does the lingering mental anguish. If these are your sufferings, remember the importance of combating any negative thoughts that may fuel this type of pain and anguish.

It's okay to feel the feeling and sit in it a while, but not for too long. Try to identify it's origin and whether it is trauma related, if you have not already done so. Learn healthy ways of coping until that pain passes and, if it continues to be an issue, please seek help to overcome it.

Other types of abuse that can result in emotional pain are childhood abuse and neglect, domestic violence, bullying, gaslighting, just to name a few. These things can negatively affect one's self-esteem, self-worth, and self-confidence. So, along with learning to cope with the emotional pain there may be a need for you to work on building your self-esteem and self-confidence.

God promises He will heal your broken heart and wounds. He desires to rebuild what the trauma has torn down.

What prayer might you pray as it relates to this type of healing?

DAY 27

DAY 28

Commit to Your Healing!

"Those things, which ye have both learned, and received, and heard, and seen in me, do: and the God of peace shall be with you."

Philippians 4:9 (KJV)

Believing you can recover is so important for healing to even be possible. The healing process takes work, and it takes time – a commitment! It will not happen overnight. You must be committed to do the work required to recover.

Think about it. How long have you been functioning in a traumatized state and experiencing out of control emotions or flashbacks or nightmares? For months, years, decades? Dysfunctional ways of thinking and being will need to be replaced which takes time. There will be good days and bad days along the way and, hopefully, the good days will overshadow the bad days.

Healing is about truly getting to know yourself, confronting your fears, identifying the signs of unresolved trauma, identifying what you need to change and the things you cannot change, how to cope, and what you need to do to become your best YOU!

Yes, Jesus is the ultimate Healer, He is Jehovah-Rapha – you must have faith that He is who He says He is. Pray and meditate on His Word. His Holy Spirit will be your guide along the way.

Have you heard the saying *"Today is the first day of the rest of your life"*? Well, it is!

What steps will you take this first day as a commitment towards your healing? It's not too late. Start today.

DAY 28

DAY 29

Knowledge is Power
*"The heart of the prudent acquires knowledge,
And the ear of the wise seeks knowledge."*

Proverbs 18:15

Learn all you can about why you do what you do, say what you say, and react the way that you do. Knowledge is power. Seek the answers to the questions you have (from a reliable source) and educate yourself about the type of trauma you have experienced and the normal responses to such a trauma. This is something you can do for you.

Learn about how rape can impact a woman mentally, physically, and spiritually. Learn about how childhood sexual abuse can affect a survivor's entire life if gone untreated. You may come to know that how it has affected you is normal and that you are not "crazy" as some may think. You may come to realize that what happened to you was *not* normal, but the way you respond because of that traumatic experience is normal. Keep in mind that trauma affects each person differently and the signs manifested through you may be different from someone who has had a similar experience.

Awareness is key. Knowledge is power. Action in necessary. So, after seeking and finding the answers to those why questions, what will you do next for your recovery?

What are the signs that you have discovered that are because of what has happened to you?

Now that you know, when will you get on your pathway to healing?

What is a first step you will take towards your healing?

Will you seek counseling for help along the way?

DAY 29

DAY 30

You May be Stronger Than You Think

"Be strong and of good courage, do not fear nor be afraid
of them; for the Lord your God, He is the One who goes
with you. He will not leave you nor forsake you."

Deuteronomy 31:6

Life can be scary and yes, you have suffered a traumatic wound. Whatever happened to you, you survived and now you can learn how to thrive! Think about that! It's your choice. On your pathway to healing and wholeness take note of your gifts and talents that can be used to help and serve others. Be aware of those things others say you are good at doing and do those things. Begin where you are and with what you have. Sometimes all it takes is to just try and if you don't know what to do, pray and ask. Prepare yourself for what lies ahead as best you can. Perhaps start with the small things and build yourself up! Remember God is with you. Despite what has happened to you, you can regain mastery over your life in some way.

It takes courage to stand up to those people who (it seems) have made it their life's mission to bring you down. As 1 Corinthian 16:13 says *"Watch, stand fast in the faith, be brave, be strong."* Begin by setting boundaries and allowing only those people who will support you when needed into your circle but who will also hold you accountable when you are wrong or heading down the wrong path.

Can you think of a time when you demonstrated your strength?

What can you do to demonstrate the strength within you?

Can you think of a time when you felt God's presence, felt that He was with you? Write about that event.

DAY 30

DAY 31

Connect Again

*"For if they fall, one will lift up his companion. But woe to him
who is alone when he falls, For he has no one to help him up."*

Ecclesiastes 4:10

Trauma, especially childhood abuse, can have a devastating effect on inter-personal relationships and the ability to form healthy bonds, especially when a parent is the abuser. Relationships are often disrupted and destroyed, trust is broken, and safety is shattered in the case of an offending caregiver, resulting in broken attachments and family dysfunction. However, relationships are important to our well-being.

Building healthy relationships and maintaining those relationships can be difficult, especially after sexual trauma. Perhaps a good way to start is by making a positive connection with at least one other person, someone you know can be trusted and build upon that foundation. We need one another and it is important to reestablish and build new and healthy relationships after trauma. A quote by Judith Herman, author of the book *Trauma and Recovery* says, "*Recovery can take place only within the context of relationships; it cannot occur in isolation.*" As you start your journey to healing, remember reconnecting with self is also important. So, come out of hiding and learn to love again, learn to live again. As you begin to live your life, you could make someone else's life better.

If you are a believer, identify a prayer partner. It can be someone who has had a similar experience, but it doesn't have to be. It could be a mother like your-self who you can pray with. You don't have to share your story with your prayer partner, that's your choice. However, a prayer partner can be a great support for the common struggles of life.

Can you think of at least two ways you can meet new people and make connections for new relationships? Can you think of at least two ways to rees-tablish an old relationship that may have been damaged because of your struggle to function in a traumatized state?

DAY 31

DAY 32

God's Grace

*"The Lord will perfect that which concerns me; Your mercy, O
Lord, endures forever; Do not forsake the works of Your hands."*

Psalm 138:8

Sometimes in life we move faster than the rate of God's grace, expecting the healing process or other things in our lives to move along a lot quicker than the time required. We must be prepared for change and patient if His process and timing is slower than we expect or hope for.

Although God promises that He will do what is said in this scripture, we must remain patient and know that because of His grace we are saved. Because of His grace and mercy we are forgiven and His grace is extended to us all even when it is undeserved.

"Perfect" in the Strong's Concordance (#1587) for this scripture verse means to complete, to make us what we ought to be. God will bring to fruition that which He has promised. He strengthens us and gives us peace.

In 2 Corinthians 12:9 Jesus says, *"My grace is sufficient for you, for My strength is made perfect in weakness."* Now I realize that during those childhood experiences it was His strength that kept me when I felt weak, helpless, and hopeless.

Know that when we are weak, He *is* strong. This is important to remember because when things that we are unable to handle happen as we go about our daily lives, we can call on Him for His help and His strength. We can pray for his continued grace and mercy.

What will be your prayer today?

DAY 32

DAY 33

Activate Your Faith

"And He said unto her, Daughter, be of good comfort:
thy faith hath made thee whole; go in peace."

Luke 8:48 (KJV)

The woman with the issue of blood had the faith to be healed. She had a flow of blood for 12 years and no "physician" could help her (Luke 8:43). She did all she knew to do but nothing worked. When she understood and believed that Jesus could heal her, He did.

When something traumatic happens our faith fades and there is a tendency for some to turn from God because of the lack of understanding as to why he would allow such a thing to happen. He does not turn away from us and He waits for us to return to Him.

There are some who would take exception to the healing in this scripture literally taking place. What do you believe? There are many scripture verses that refer to people believing and then being healed. I'm sure there have been times when you've prayed for the healing of a loved one and your prayers were answered. Then again you may have prayed for another, and that prayer was not answered the way you had hoped. I wondered why my younger sister passed away from cancer leaving three young children behind, although many prayed for her recovery. I've often wondered, does healing require the person in need of healing to have the faith to be healed? We may never know.

As I've said and believe, and as difficult as it may be to accept, everything happens for a reason. Regardless, we must have faith. What I do know and believe is that my sister is now healed in the *"house not made with hands"* – Heaven (2 Corinthians 5:1) where she no longer suffers and is no longer in pain.

Remember His thoughts are not our thoughts and His ways are not our ways (Isaiah 55:8). So why mention the woman with the issue of blood? So that we will remember that healing *is* possible. And perhaps you know someone who has been healed through prayer. Do you?

DAY 33

DAY 34

From Broken to Mended
"And I will restore to you the years that the locust hath
eaten, the cankerworm, and the caterpillar, and the
palmerworm, my great army which I sent among you."

Joel 2:25 (KJV)

In their early stages these insects must crawl through the dirt and mud, struggling just to survive. This is what it may seem like as a trauma survivor. The damage has been done and you are feeling broken. Relationships have been destroyed or damaged and the sense of safety lost. Now what? God promises He will restore those years that were ruined. That could mean new relationships formed or the old renewed.

There are people from our past who have betrayed us and who could remain a threat to our mental wellbeing. These people should be identified as triggers. Although God expects us to forgive, He does not require us to continue those relationships and keep ourselves in harm's way.

God promises to retore our years of brokenness and release our minds from bondage. He wants to put those tattered pieces together and mend our broken hearts. All we need do is ask *and* believe.

From our broken state God can mend us and transform us into the people He would have us to be, working from the inside out. We may not see it, we may not feel it, but He is at work while we wait in faith to be restored – mind, body, and spirit. But in the waiting, we must continue to do what we know to do. Pray? Meditate on His Word? Praise Him? While taking time to also *"Be still, and know that [He is] God,"* Psalm 46:10.

What is it that you can do while you wait on the Lord to restore those years and mend your broken heart?

DAY 34

DAY 35

The Courage to Heal

*"Have I not commanded you? Be strong and of good
courage; do not be afraid, nor be dismayed, for the
Lord your God is with you wherever you go."*

Joshua 1:9

My journey of recovery from child abuse was long and hard. I cried many tears, faced many fears, listened to wise counsel, read the Word and prayed all along the way. And, once I discovered what God's purpose was for my life and began to walk in it, my life began to change for the better.

Life continues to have its ups and downs, but I know and have always known that I am not alone. I believe all things will work together for good just like is said in Romans 8:28. You too are not alone for God is with you. I have asked Him to let me feel His presence and He has many times. If it worked for me, it can work for you. Isn't it worth asking?

It takes courage to get on that road to recovery from trauma. It can be scary at times. It takes hard work and commitment to heal. God promises He will never make us ashamed (Romans 10:11). Not you, not me. He is the one who can free you from the bondage of life gone by. He is our deliverer, but you must want to be delivered and set free.

You must have the courage to heal and the desire to be made whole. It won't be easy, but it will be worth the effort. You must have faith and believe healing is even possible.

Do you believe you can be healed? What will be your first step on your pathway to healing?

DAY 35

DAY 36

Resilience: Bounce Back

"We are hard-pressed on every side, yet not crushed; we are perplexed, but not in despair; persecuted, but not forsaken; struck down, but not destroyed-"

2 Corinthians 4:8-9

Resilience is what I call the bounce back factor. It's one's ability to bounce back from whatever has created a stumbling block along life's journey. Resiliency can be compromised when someone experiences a traumatic event. Some people are more resilient than others after trauma and are able to bounce back a lot quicker than those with a lower level of resilience.

If a traumatic experience goes unaddressed and then something else traumatic happens, the resiliency level is compromised even more making it even more difficult to bounce back. But with help you can rebuild your level of resilience and learn how to remain strong should something else occur.

Identify a support system of people you trust, can confide in, and call on when you need help. Support could also include getting help from a professional who can teach you coping strategies and help you to build your level of resilience and self-confidence.

Keeping yourself physically and mentally healthy can help maintain resiliency as well as being able to identify support when problems arise. It's important to know your strengths now so that you can draw upon those strengths when trouble occurs. It's also important not to give up. God will make a way when there seems to be no way.

What is it that you need to do to regain your strength to bounce back from your traumatic experience?

DAY 36

DAY 37

Reclaim your Voice
"Unless the Lord had been my help, My soul
would soon have settled in silence."

Psalm 94:17

This scripture is so true for my life. Because of the traumatic childhood I experienced, I lost my voice. I was introverted, quiet and afraid. When I told what was happening to me, I was not believed so I didn't tell again, and the abuse continued. If I did not believe that the Lord heard my cries, helped me, and guided me along the way, I would not have regained my voice nor started my journey to wholeness. Because of Him I am free and am now able to assert myself, stand up for the rights of others and encourage and teach other women how to speak up for themselves.

There are three Tamar's mentioned in the Bible. Tamar, the daughter of King David, was raped by her half-brother Amnon who went unpunished by their father, King David (2 Samuel Chapter 13). Tamar's cries and screams were ignored as her brother had his way with her. After the trauma of it all, she was silenced, disregarded, and unheard except by her brother Absalom who cared for her for a time after. However, she lost her voice and hid in shame. I hope that this will not be the end of your story.

Reclaim your voice! Talk, talk, talk about it, at first with an entrusted professional or a trusted friend who will listen and empathize. Talking about what happened to you is part of the healing process and could give you a sense of relief. Keeping things bottled up is not good. Eventually, after you've shared a while, you may notice you no longer become emotional if you continue to share.

Sometimes a listening ear and being believed is all you need. Find that someone.

DAY 37

DAY 38

The Need for Peace

*"Peace I leave with you, My peace I give to you: not as the world gives, do
I give to you. Let not your heart be troubled, neither let it be afraid."*

John 14:27

After trauma, there is often the quest for a sense of peace. You may feel
that your life is out of control because of the fear that lingers, the flashbacks, the
nightmares, and memories of what happened to you. Once you become aware of
the connection between your way of responding to everyday situations – what
you say, how you feel, and what you do - and the trauma you have experienced
you may feel a sense of peace, at least a sense of relief because you now know why.

Being aware, in the *knowing*, you can now do something about it. Now
that you are aware of the root cause for your rage, out of control emotions and
the need to withdraw from others you can get the help you've needed for so long.
Hopefully you will do just that.

I know what it's like not knowing. For years, I had no idea why I became
depressed for long periods of time, why I dissociated so often, why I was so confused, and did not know anything about triggers. I knew something was wrong
but didn't know what was wrong.

I heard a young woman tell her story on a Christian TV show which was
very similar to my own. Then a sense of peace came over me and I knew what I
had to do to get well. I felt the peace of God that *"surpasses all understanding"*
(Philippians 4:7) and knew I was going to be okay. This was the beginning of my
healing journey. Knowing *why* I was in the state I was in was life changing. As I
took those steps toward healing, I came to know what God's purpose is for my
life. It is to help you!

Why are you in the state that you are in?

DAY 38

DAY 39

Worry No More

"Be anxious for nothing, but in everything by prayer and supplication, with thanksgiving, let your request be made known to God; and the peace of God, which surpasses all understanding will guard your hearts and minds through Christ Jesus."

Philippians 4:6-7

Worry can be caused by stress and stress can lead to physical health problems and trigger active negative thoughts. These thoughts can become out of control and begin racing in your mind. Unfortunately, anxiousness, nervousness, uneasiness, and fear all come with the territory after trauma. Hopefully by now you know and understand why you are feeling this way. You must gain control of your thoughts and not allow these thoughts to control you.

If there is a connection between these thoughts and past trauma, remind yourself that it is not happening now, you are safe (hopefully) and that those things are in the past. You can also pray for relief from these negative emotions, and God will relieve you of these things, as you patiently wait on Him to manifest your healing.

Relaxing your body can help relax your mind. Try calming and relaxing exercises when you start to feel anxious and stressed. You may recall the controlled breathing exercise which is taking deep breaths in and slowly breathing out until you feel a sense of calm. There are various ways of doing this exercise. You can do an easy web search to find the one that works best for you. Often positive self-talk works, especially when done consistently. Listening to music may also help. For instance, listening to CeCe Winans' song called *"Peace From God,"* can provide comfort when you are struggling.

What will be your prayer today for relief from anxiety, nervousness, uneasiness, and fear?

DAY 39

DAY 40

Nightmares

*"When you lie down, you will not be afraid; Yes, you
will lie down and your sleep will be sweet."*

Proverbs 3:24

Nightmares often interrupt sleep for a time after trauma. There may be something that you have seen, heard, smelled, touched, or even tasted during your day which triggered memories of the horrific things that have happened to you which could cause the nightmares.

You may not even be aware that you were triggered during your day, but those things can come back to you as you sleep. Make note of those things that trigger memories or flashbacks so that you can find ways to avoid or cope with them in the future.

Wouldn't it be wonderful to have a peaceful night's sleep without nightmares? Try to imagine having fun, happy times, peaceful dreams before you go to bed each night. Perhaps meditating on this scripture or developing a mantra to recite or listening to calming music before bedtime could help alleviate those nightmares. It's worth a try.

If you could create your own dreams, what would they include? Try meditating on Proverbs 3:24 to see if your dreams will be of good things. And when you are awake, think of good things. Sweet dreams!

What will you do during your day to help you sleep peacefully at night?

DAY 40

DAY 41

Shame and Self-Blame

*"Let them be ashamed and confounded together that
seek after my soul to destroy it; let them be driven
backward and put to shame that wish me evil."*

Psalm 40:14 (KJV)

They should be ashamed not you. Those who have hurt you, abused you, committed shameful acts against you, said things about you falsely, and attempted to destroy you with their words. These things may have caused you to feel less than, to see yourself in a negative way, as unlovable even to the point of self-hatred and, in some cases, cause you to self-harm. They should be ashamed for what they have done to you. Just as the above verse says they should be *"driven backward and put to shame,"* not you! You are not the one to be blamed.

Unfortunately, the victim is often made to feel ashamed and blamed for the horrific acts committed against them. I hope that you are able to comprehend that these things were *done to you*, you did not do anything to bring it upon yourself. It was not your fault. Take a minute to think about that.

As a survivor you may think, "if only I had done something different" to justify your feelings of guilt, shame, and self-blame. If you were a child and sexually abused, you must remember that you were defenseless, helpless, vulnerable, and afraid and did what was expected of you in order to survive. As an adult, these thoughts and feelings should be challenged for elimination. I say again, it was not your fault. If you were the victim of domestic violence, you probably felt the same in isolation. Reach out for help from someone you trust or a counselor to help you to work through this.

What will you do to stop that negative self-talk? Name at least 3 positive self-affirmations that you can recite daily to begin to view yourself in a more positive light.

DAY 41

DAY 42

Painful Memories

"For behold, I create new heavens and a new earth; And the former shall not be remembered nor come to mind."

Isaiah 65:17

Memories of past trauma may be triggered very easily for you right now. Do you know what triggers these painful traumatic memories? It's important to know your triggers, as has been mentioned, so that you can either avoid them or learn how to cope when this occurs. I cannot stress enough that it is important for you to remind yourself that those things are not happening to you right now. They are behind you, in your past and (hopefully) you are safe now.

God has brought you out of that for a reason. Try looking to the future and the good things He has in store for you. Make new memories, good memories. Make a continued effort to think about the good memories and not the bad memories of the past. God promises to guide you out of the wilderness and give you water in the dry places of your life (Isaiah 43:19) and make new things.

The wilderness could be those tough times you experience in the valley as you travel on your journey to wholeness. Those places where you feel lost and alone. Make every effort to get through those rough patches. Remember God is with you and will help you.

Identify at least 3 people, places or things that could trigger painful memories. Will you avoid them or learn how to cope?

Can you identify a few recent good memories?

What can you do to create new, good memories?

DAY 42

DAY 43

The Battlefield of the Mind
"Casting down imaginations, and every high thing that exalteth itself against the knowledge of God, and bringing into captivity every thought to the obedience of Christ . . ."

2 Corinthians 10:5 (KJV)

During a traumatic event, the mind's fight, flight or freeze response is activated. For me, as a child, I could not fight, I could not flee, therefore I froze and had to endure the repeated abuse throughout my childhood. I did tell but was not believed. So, imagine the impact this experience had on my child mind. Or perhaps you know from your own experience.

Not only are there mental wounds from trauma it can also deeply affect the body and spirit. It can leave a person with heightened anxiety, feeling depressed more often than the average person, fearful, being easily startled, constantly being on guard and a lack of ability to control emotions.

After trauma can also come confusion. It's normal to be confused about what happened to you. It's difficult to make sense of what has happened, especially when the abuser is a caregiver. Trying to make sense of it all on your own could cause you to feel even more confused. So, seeking the help of a professional who may be able to help you sort it all out and teach you how to challenge any negative thoughts you may be experiencing may be the next step for you.

Bring your thoughts into alignment with what God says. Asking for help is a sign of strength not weakness and it could change your life for the better.

Will you reach out for help? If so, when? Hold yourself accountable.

DAY 43

DAY 44

Renew Your Mind

*"And do not be conformed to this world, but be transformed
by the renewing of your mind, that you may prove what is
that good and acceptable and perfect will of God."*

Romans 12:2

Yes, now renew your mind. Damage has been done, but – in most cases – there can be a healing of the mind. The aftereffects of trauma can be like being held captive in your own mind and needing to be set free. Some people have a negative mindset by nature and a tendency to automatically lean towards the negative most of the time. Others focus more on the positive, the possibility of good in every situation. But after trauma this is difficult to do, and the mind must be renewed.

Some of the assignments of the Holy Spirit are to help us, guide us and teach us how to renew our minds. He will lead us and let us know what to do through prayer and meditation upon the Word. Being washed by the water of the Word (Ephesians 5:26) will begin to renew your mind. As you are being transformed (your mind renewed), God's purpose for your life will become clear and eventually will be revealed. And, walking in that purpose will change you and those you encounter, even strangers and your life will not be the same. God is working on you as you help and serve others. As your mind is being renewed you will begin to think clearer, feel better, feel stronger and become more in control of your emotions.

It will take time. No worries, God will never give up on you, so don't give up on yourself and keep your focus on Him! Pray that the Holy Spirit will renew your mind so that you will know what God's purpose is for your life as it is being revealed to you. Believe what God says about you.

Have you gotten any clues about what your life purpose is? Note them here.

DAY 44

DAY 45

Become Grounded

*"... that you, being rooted and grounded in love ... to
know the love of Christ which passes knowledge, that
you may be filled with all the fullness of God."*

Ephesians 3:17, 19

Try this exercise: go outside barefoot and walk around your yard or in the park or someplace where you can feel the ground, the earth under your feet; or on a beach where you can feel the sand running through your toes. This will help you become grounded, being in touch with the earth. How does it feel?

Another form of grounding which is to help trauma survivors remain in the present, when inside or outside, is to use the 5 senses. Using the 5 senses can bring you back to the here and now when you are triggered for a trauma response. (You can also use the 5 senses for *identifying* triggers.) You may need someone to help you with this by first calling out your name.

Here is a well-known grounding technique using the 5 senses: name 5 things you can see and describe each, name 4 things you can touch and touch each; name 3 things you can hear; name 2 things you can taste; name 1 thing you can smell. This naming of things using the 5 senses can be switched around and used in whatever order works best for you. The purpose is to bring your focus back to the present, after being triggered, for a sense of safety.

You can also memorize scripture to recite and meditate on when triggered to become rooted and grounded in God's Word.

Have you identified your triggers? Which grounding technique will you use when you are triggered?

DAY 45

DAY 46

Be Empowered

*"Finally, my brethren, be strong in the Lord
and in the power of His might."*

Ephesians 6:10

Abuse is about power and control, the taking of someone's power and forcing control. It can also be restricting someone's ability to make choices for themselves or to move around freely.

After trauma there can be self-doubt, dislike of self, lack of self-confidence, an inability to assert self and being unable to trust others. After trauma you may also feel powerless and unable to make right choices. If the trauma you experienced is in the past and you are currently safe and out of harm's way, you are no longer a victim, you are a survivor, and on your way to thriving! You can now take control of your life. Remember God is with you to empower you to become strong.

Being empowered, at least in part, is recognizing you have the power to make your own choices and making them, the right to speak up for yourself (using your voice), the courage to be confident, being self-aware and being able to maintain control over your own destiny.

Knowing what makes you happy, being your best self, identifying your goals and pursuing them, as well as helping others can also be empowering.

But these things are difficult to do after experiencing something tragic and which may need to be relearned. Self-empowerment is part of the healing process and means taking back control of your life. It's self-care, learning to love yourself and others again.

What steps will you take today to become empowered?

DAY 46

DAY 47

Be Safe

""I will both lie down in peace, and sleep; For You
alone, O Lord, make me dwell in safety."

Psalm 4:8

As you start your journey toward healing, being safe and a sense of safety are important. If you are in an abusive relationship with a spouse or partner, create a plan for safety whether you decide you want to stay or in preparation for leaving. Be sure to identify your support system for contact, have quick access to emergency numbers, and identify a place where you will be safe.

If you have been able to escape an abusive relationship, I applaud your courage and strength! (Hallelujah!) Hopefully you are now safe. Now is the time for you to get started on your pathway to healing and get help to recover if this experience was traumatic for you.

It's important to identify the red flags you may have ignored in the past and learn how to set healthy boundaries (personal, emotional, and sexual) so that you can avoid similar situations and unhealthy relationships.

RAINN (Rape, Abuse and Incest National Network) has safety planning tips on their website at www.rainn.org/articles/safety-planning. There you will find safety tips for the following situations: when someone is hurting you; when someone is stalking you; and when leaving the person who is hurting you.

Remember to look to God in prayer, believing in His power to keep you safe.

Now may be a good time to develop your safety plan, if you have not done so in the past.

DAY 47

DAY 48

Does Everything Happen for a Reason?

"For My thoughts are not your thoughts, Nor are your ways My ways,"
says the Lord. For as the heavens are higher than the earth, So are My
ways higher than your ways, And My thoughts than your thoughts."

Isaiah 55:8-9

God knows all from the beginning to the end as it relates to our lives and all things. The way He thinks is different from the way we think. His way of doing things is absolutely different from our way. We, on the other hand, may never know the answers to the why questions we have about the horrific things that have happened to us.

Does everything happen for a reason? Some may not believe this to be true, but what if there is a reason for the good and bad things that happen? Some reasons may be revealed to us here in this earthly realm; some may be revealed when we join our Creator.

Does why really matter? We can't go back and undo the past. Even if we were able to go back, we wouldn't have the knowledge we have today needed to avoid, fix or do things differently. I can think of only one reason knowing why would be to our advantage. We could learn something helpful from whatever that thing is.

We *can* live for today and look forward to and hope for a better future. We *can* work towards a better tomorrow by taking care of ourselves and our loved ones and doing the difficult things we need to do to heal the wounds of the past.

How important is it to you to know the answer to your why questions?

Why?

DAY 48

DAY 49

Moving Beyond Traumatic Fear

"I sought the Lord, and He heard me, and delivered me from all my fears."

Psalm 34:4

Healthy fear is fear that helps us *avoid* danger. It keeps us safe. For instance, when children are told not to touch a hot stove because it could burn them. This is instilling a healthy fear. It keeps children from being burned. When warned, most children would then be afraid to touch a hot stove and avoid it.

Then there is traumatic fear. What I call "traumatic fear" is fear that triggers the fight, flight, freeze response immediately before a traumatic event, during a traumatic event and the lingering fear after. When something frightens us, a quick reaction is to run or fight. If we are prevented from running and cannot fight, we freeze. After the event traumatic fear can be triggered by memories, nightmares, or flashbacks.

Traumatic events can produce a fear of people who remind you of the abuser/perpetrator, a fear of traveling to new places, a fear of trusting others, being afraid to trust yourself and disrupts a sense of safety. After trauma fear can exist even when there is no apparent reason to be afraid. This kind of fear is a heavy burden that survivors carry with them wherever they go until they decide to confront it.

This type of fear can also keep you isolated, keep you from doing the things you enjoy and have a desire to do and keep you from living life to the fullest. However, it is possible to overcome this type of fear. Perhaps a friend or a professional can help you break through that fear. Pray about when you should confront a particular fear (in a safe manner).

What are your fears resulting from the traumatic things that have happened to you? Will you pray about whether it is time for you to confront these fears and how to prepare for it?

DAY 49

DAY 50

Suffer From That Thing No More

"For I consider that the sufferings of this present time are not worthy to be compared with the glory which shall be revealed in us."

Romans 8:18

God is waiting to help you. All you need do is ask and believe He will do what He says He will do, although in His time. He says in Isaiah 40:31 *"But those that wait upon the LORD shall renew their strength; . . . they shall run and not be weary, they shall walk and not faint,"* and in 3 John 1:2 *"Beloved, I pray that you may prosper in all things and be in health, just as your soul prospers."*

Overcoming the pain, suffering and distress after trauma can take time and a desire to do so. You must be patient. First, being aware of the way you respond to a given situation, the heightened emotional responses, the harsh words that come from your mouth and the rage is important.

Next, being aware that the cause of behaviors and inner turmoil is most likely that thing, that pivotal event that changed your life forever. Refuse to allow it to keep you stuck and hold you captive. Yes, take time to grieve and mourn that which has been lost but, please, move on from it. The trauma we have suffered cannot be compared to the great works that will be revealed in and through us (Romans 8:18).

Wake up, sit up, stand up and think about the good days ahead. As you ask, seek and pray, the purpose God has for your life will be revealed. His Spirit will work in you and through you.

What will your fist step be?

DAY 50

DAY 51

Release the Resentment and Bitterness That Lingers
*"Let all bitterness, wrath, anger, clamor, and evil
speaking be put away from you, with all malice."*

Ephesians 4:31

When we harbor negative emotions for long periods of time, these emotions affect us not only mentally but can begin to affect us physically. After trauma there is a tendency to hold on to resentment, bitterness, and anger or rage, and to engage in evil speaking, especially when memories of the traumatic events are triggered.

Why? The anger could be because of the helplessness and being trapped, with no way of escape during the horrific event. The bitterness could stem from the fact that those who should have protected you and kept you safe were instead your abusers. The lingering resentment because those who could have done something and should have done something, simply stood by pretending to be blind to what was happening around them. I know, because it happened to me but what released me from these negative emotions was remembering Jesus said, *"Father, forgive them; for they know not what they do (Luke 23:34)."*

Holding on to negative emotions can keep you stuck and hold you back from living your life to the fullest. While you are engaging in unhealthy thoughts that provoke these negative feelings and behaviors, in some cases, the offenders are living their lives as though they have done nothing wrong, as though nothing ever happened. A quote from Nelson Mandela says, *"Resentment is like drinking poison and then hoping it will kill your enemies."*

I hope you will work to replace those seeds of intense anger, bitterness and resentment and replace them with seeds of love, forgiveness, joy, and peace. What will you do to banish these negative emotions? What is your prayer in this regard?

DAY 51

DAY 52

When Feeling Abandoned

"When my father and my mother forsake me,
Then the LORD will take care of me."

Psalm 27:10

Abusers can be parents who could cause a child to feel lost and lonely. Children can feel abandoned when placed in foster care or adopted, but also when living in the home with their biological parents feeling abandoned emotionally. For a child being abandoned is difficult to comprehend, and it can be like years of wandering in the wilderness, unless another adult steps up and attempts to make up for what has been lost. If this is you, remember God was with you then and He is with you now.

For me just having the *knowing* that God was with me throughout my traumatic childhood is what gave me hope and helped me to survive. They who caused me harm meant it for evil, but God meant it for good as said in Genesis 50:20.

If it had not been for what happened to me, I would not have been able to help other women on their pathway to healing who suffer from traumatic experiences much like my own. It was because of this I have had that privilege. So, I am grateful and blessed to have been able to help others along the way through His purpose for my life.

When memories come and that feeling of loneliness strikes, remember God will never leave you nor forsake you. And, cherish those who are with you now.

Other than our Savior, can you name at least one person who helped you through some trying time? It could have been a teacher, a co-worker, a boss, or even a stranger.

DAY 52

DAY 53

From Rejection to Acceptance
"If the world hates you, you know that it hated Me before it hated you."

John 15:18

Jesus was hated because the people of His day did not believe He *is* who He says He *is* and they resented His saying so. Too bad for them! So, when people hate you, dislike you, reject you because of what others have said about you falsely, too bad for them too! They don't know the real you. It's their loss because God has begun a good work in you (Philippians 1:6) and He is not done with you yet!

Although it feels good to be accepted, it may be a waste of time to try and get people to like you, especially when you strive to be your best self and have done no harm to them. It could be more about them and their insecurities or jealousy then it is about you. On a recent holiday TV show Dolly Parton (love her) spoke about how she loves everyone and wants everyone to love her. But what stuck with me was when she said, *"The people who love me make up for the people who don't."* Not everyone is going to love or like you! And it's okay because the people who love you overshadow those who don't.

Because of what you have been through, you may be more susceptible to feelings of rejection. Feeling rejected can cause you to become depressed and cause you to isolate; therefore, it is important to know how to cope with rejection from others and how to be accepting of yourself. You may find acceptance from people who have similar interests, people who are supportive and accepting of your kindness.

If your focus is on trying to get people to like you, it could be a distraction from doing what God has planned for you to do. People believe what they want to believe and may believe what others say about you even when the things said are untrue; even when they have not taken the time to get to know you for themselves.

What is your plan to work through this?

DAY 53

DAY 54

The Fruit of the Spirit

*"But the fruit of the Spirit is love, joy, peace, longsuffering,
kindness, goodness, faithfulness, gentleness, self-control."*

Galatians 5:22-23

After trauma, emotional responses are often heightened. Instead of self-control there can be a lack of the ability to control one's emotions. Anger can become rage. Joy turns to sadness. Peace turns to conflict driven fear, and love and kindness are replaced with hatred and resentment. These emotions need to be turned around. Counseling can help survivors learn how to manage these inappropriate emotional responses.

We can make an effort to walk in the Spirit. This scripture verse can be a guide. Of course, this is not an easy thing to do. After all we are only human and imperfect beings. However, we can do our best to express the fruit of the Spirit in our lives with the help of the Holy Spirit. Philippians 4:13 says that we *"can do all things through Christ who strengthens [us]."* We can learn longsuffering, self-control, how to love again, express kindness and find joy; all the fruit of the Holy Spirit.

Pick one fruit of the Spirit you will focus on and express.

Which one do you choose today?

Choose one each day to focus on and express, or one each week to see the difference it can make in your life and that of others.

DAY 54

DAY 55

Self-Care

*"Or do you not know that your body is the temple of the Holy
Spirit who is in you, whom you have from God, and you are
not your own? For you were bought at a price; therefore glorify
God in your body and in your spirit, which are God's."*

1 Corinthians 6:19-20

Pay attention to YOU – it is difficult to help others if you don't take care of
and help yourself! Check in with yourself daily to see if you are okay and, if not,
know what you can do to help yourself feel better. Are you getting enough sleep
and eating healthy meals? What about exercise to keep yourself fit? We are made
in God's image and His Spirit dwells within us, even more of a reason we should
take care of ourselves.

Do you need help because you are struggling with out-of-control emotions,
feeling depressed, or feeling overwhelmed? If so, reach out and seek the help you
need. Maybe talking to a trusted friend or trusted family member could help. As
a trauma survivor, you may need to seek help from a professional.

In the meantime, do what you can do to take care of yourself. Do something
fun, something that makes you feel happy, something that makes you laugh. Relax
and eat some ice cream (that's my favorite) but not too much, take time for a
bubble bath (another favorite), engage in hobbies, or do something fun with your
children. Schedule times to do these things and do them at least one time a week.
This also gives you something to look forward to. The mere thought of having
something exciting to look forward to can conjure up good feelings.

What will you do to ensure you are taking good care of yourself?

List at least 5 things you can do to make yourself feel better. How often will
you do these things and when?

DAY 55

DAY 56

Self-Esteem and Self-Confidence

*"Therefore do not cast away your confidence, which has great
reward. For you have need of endurance, so that after you have
done the will of God, you may receive the promise: . . ."*

Hebrews 10:35-36

Self-esteem is how you feel about yourself. Self-confidence is the confidence you have in your ability to do different things. A traumatic experience, especially sexual trauma (control of the body) and domestic violence (control of the body and mind), can be detrimental to a person's self-esteem and self-confidence.

Learning to feel good about oneself, being confident in your abilities and strengths after trauma is important to the healing process. There is a need to learn how to love yourself. Knowing the things you like about you, the things you dislike, knowing the things you can change, accepting the things you cannot change (like the Serenity Prayer states) is a good place to start.

After trauma we can be our own worst enemy with our negative self-talk, self-blame, guilt, being self-conscious, and ashamed. After sexual abuse you may even feel damaged, unclean, and wanting to escape your own body. These emotions and behaviors need to be addressed for your sake, so that you can move forward and do what God has planned for your life. As this verse says, *"do not cast away your confidence which has great reward."* There are people waiting for you to help them along the way.

What are some things you do well? Yes, you do something well.

What are some things you are confident you are good at doing? If you are unsure, ask a friend. Learn ways to build your confidence.

Name at least 3 accomplishments from your past.

DAY 56

DAY 57

Know What Makes You Happy
"A merry heart does good, like medicine, But
a broken spirit dries the bones."

Proverbs 17:22

I was watching America's Got Talent one night. I love watching that show. It activates every emotion within me as I listen to the contestants sing from their hearts and do what they do. When they share their stories it causes me to feel sad to the point of bringing tears to my eyes but the acts have also made me smile and laugh until my sides hurt.

This night, a woman named Jane Marczewski ("Nightbirde") came on stage and mentioned that she had been dealing with terminal cancer for a few years, and when asked how she is now she named the parts of her body where the cancer remains. However, she expressed she is waiting for her miracle! Then, she sang, with a beautiful voice a song called *"It's Okay"* (which she had written) that brought tears to my eyes. (You can see her singing that song on youtube.) After singing, with hope in her voice, she made this profound statement *"You can't wait until life isn't hard anymore before you decide to be happy."* Take a minute to think about that keeping in mind that life has its ups and downs. It seems Jane stepped out in faith to sing on America's Got Talent because it made her happy to be able to do something that would bring joy to so many others.

Your spirit may have been broken because of life experiences, but it can be put back together again. Life's hard times does not mean we can't find happiness in the midst of it all. You can find happiness by traveling to a place you enjoy, doing something you like or spending time with a person you like. Not that someone else can *make* you happy. But just being around certain people can make us feel happy.

So, what makes you happy? Take the time to enjoy those things.

DAY 57

DAY 58

It's a Struggle
"For I, the Lord your God, will hold your right hand,
saying to you, 'Fear not, I will help you.'"

Isaiah 41:13

On your pathway to healing it will not be easy and healing takes time. God promises throughout His Word that He will help you. There will be ups and downs, twists and turns, grief and loss, good days, and bad days. You will need help along the way. All you need do is ask. Remember, asking for help is not a sign of weakness but a sign of strength.

Your response to what happened *is normal*, what happened to you is what *is abnormal*. After trauma it is important to reconnect, not only with the world and others, but with your true self. Because God created us to help one another, He will send people your way who will be of help to you.

Do you believe He will help you as He says He will? Search the Word for yourself to increase your faith in Him. He says that we will have tribulations (difficulties) but that He has overcome the world (John 16:33). He is with you to help you through it all.

If you are thinking "Well, I've done this," or "I've done that," remember *all* have sinned and fallen short (Romans 3:23). No one is perfect, and God is forgiving. I would not have made it without Him. First John 4:4 says *"greater is He that is in you, than he that is in the world,"* so, you will overcome.

Is there anything for which you need forgiveness? Will you pray for forgiveness? Will you pray for the help that you need?

DAY 58

DAY 59

The Power of a Hug
"In the multitude of my anxieties within me,
Your comforts delight my soul."

Psalm 94:19

In the days before I knew the affect that child abuse and domestic violence had upon me, I would experience bouts of deep depression. When I became depressed, I isolated myself from others, spent long hours in bed, and did only what was necessary for survival. I felt like a robot just going through the motions to sustain life.

During those times my daughter would say to me "Mom, I need a hug." She said this not because *she* needed a hug, but because she knew I was the one who needed a hug. This small gesture was huge for me at the time. It made her happy too. It helped me make it through those sad and lonely days, and I felt loved.

Those hugs were powerful and gave me a stronger desire to hold on until healing was manifested through me. It was a reminder to me that someone cared. That's the power of a hug.

I wish I could suggest giving hugs, but I can't since we all are suffering from the social mandates limiting contact because of the pandemic. So, it is not advised to give hugs to strangers at this time, and we should use caution when deciding to hug a family member living outside of our homes. Bummer ☹!

Nevertheless, God will comfort you whenever you need.

DAY 59

DAY 60

Hope in the Midst of it All

*"Be of good courage, And He shall strengthen your
heart, All you who hope in the Lord."*

Psalm 31:24

The Merriam-Webster dictionary defines hope as *"to want something to happen or be true and think that it could happen or be true."* Hope and faith go together. Hebrews 11:1 says, *"Now faith is the substance of things hoped for, the evidence of things not seen."* Faith is the belief that the thing hoped for will come into existence.

Hope is the unseen as Romans 8:24 says: *". . . hope that is seen is not hope; for why does one still hope for what he sees?"* Hope puts us in the waiting stage and the need to trust that God will do what He says He will do. Experiencing hope after trauma is not easy, it takes faith, strong faith. We hope that things will get better. We need God's help to keep us lifted up as we wait for the things hoped for.

Hope in the midst of it all is, most importantly, our hope in God as we move forward in faith. For hope in the future, hope for positive change, place your hope in Him. He will help keep us lifted and looking forward to the good He has in store for us.

So, why not pray for peace, pray for courage, and pray for strength as you start your healing journey.

What gives you hope? What is your hope for tomorrow?

DAY 60

DAY 61

Be an Agent of Change

*"Those from among you will build the old waste places; You shall
raise up the foundations of many generations; And you shall be called
the Repairer of the Breach, The Restorer of Streets to Dwell In."*

Isaiah 58:12

Acts of abuse and neglect are often repeated in families from generation to generation. When you think about it, has there been abuse, neglect, abandonment, domestic violence in your family in times past? With help, you can learn to be the agent of change in your family and break that cycle of abuse. You can begin to break the generational curse and become *"the Repairer of the Breach* and *the Restorer of Streets."* ("Streets" in this verse means paths.) If your family is free of intergenerational trauma, please remain diligent to prevent the cycle from beginning.

Childhood sexual abuse, when committed by a family member, often remains a secret within the family and no one tells. When no one tells this secret leaves the door open for the abuse to continue. You can be instrumental in breaking that cycle, first by protecting your own children and then speaking up for yourself.

If you are struggling to successfully parent *your* children because of the trauma you have suffered as a child, help is available. You can learn how to help yourself and how to keep your children safe from harm. This is a part of becoming an agent of change.

Once you get the help you need through therapy and trauma informed parenting classes, and as you learn new ways of thinking and being, you can be the change that you and your children need.

What can you do to become the agent of change in your family?

DAY 61

DAY 62

It's Never Too Late

*". . . being confident of this very thing, that He who has begun a
good work in you will complete it until the day of Jesus Christ:"*

Philippians 1:6

I consider myself to be a late bloomer. After graduating from high school, I did not know what I wanted to do or was meant to do. I was like the Israelites wandering in the wilderness for years. I was not living; I was merely existing. I was wandering unknowingly in a traumatized state until I heard the testimony of the woman, I spoke of earlier, whose childhood experience was like mine.

This woman spoke of how the Lord led her to seek "wise counsel" and as she began to heal her life purpose was discovered. As she continued to share her story, it clicked, and I knew then what I was meant to do. So, after working for many years in a job I absolutely hated I returned to school and obtained the degrees I needed to pursue a career in counseling. I am not telling you this to toot my own horn, but to help you see that if God was willing to do it for me, He can and will do it for you. I am special in His sight and so are YOU!

It's never too late to pursue your dreams. It's never too late to fulfill God's purpose for your life. Luke 19:13 says that we are to *"occupy till [He] comes,"* which means to keep doing what God has for you to do until Jesus comes.

As Paul says in this scripture, I hope you are confident that God, *"who has begun a good work in you will complete it."* It's never too late!

Is there something you have wanted to do but thought it was too late? Does it line up with God's purpose for your life? Will you pursue it?

DAY 62

DAY 63

Beauty From the Ashes

*"To console those who mourn in Zion, To give them beauty for
ashes, The oil of joy for mourning, The garment of praise for the
spirit of heaviness; That they may be called trees of righteousness,
The planting of the Lord, that He may be glorified."*

Isaiah 61:3

What comes to mind when you think of ashes? What comes to mind when
you think of beauty? Ashes remind me of death as when a person is cremated. The
word beauty causes me to think of the beauty of nature, of all the beautiful things
the Lord has made, including us.

A person's beauty can be seen on the outside and felt when they express it
from the inside. Beauty on the inside can last a lifetime but beauty on the outside
is fading. I believe the beauty referred to in this verse is the inside kind.

The word Zion has many meanings. According to Strong's Concordance
(#H6726) of the Bible, it means "a parched place." You may believe you are in a
parched place because of the things that were done to you and the things people
say about you. Remember God promises to *"restore to you the years that the locust
hath eaten, the cankerworm, and the caterpillar, and the palmerworm" (Joel 2:25
KJV)* and He will. When you are restored, the ashes will fade away, the beauty
will come forth and you will feel renewed.

Lauren Daigle in her song entitled *"You Say,"* disputes the negative things
we say about ourselves and puts into this song what God says about us – good
things – and reminds us of who we are in Christ.

Give it a listen and journal the thoughts and feelings that come up for you
after listening to this song.

DAY 63

DAY 64

God's Purpose for Your Life

"There are many plans in a man's heart, Nevertheless
the Lord's counsel—that will stand."

Proverbs 19:21

We were created to do good works. God knew before we were born what He would have us do. He will guide us, but it is up to us to figure out what that is. Become aware of the things you are good at doing and how those things benefit others. Focus on those things you are able to do that come easily for you and that perhaps you can do better than others. Think about the different spiritual gifts listed in 1 Corinthians 12:4-10 and Romans 12:6-8. These are the gifts to be used for the benefit of others in love. But in the exercising of these gifts, I believe it will bring to you happiness, joy, and peace. Once you discover what God's purpose is for your life and you begin to walk in it, your life will never be the same for the better.

Romans 12 lists some of these different gifts as serving, teaching, encouraging, giving generously, to lead, to show mercy. There are many ways to express and share these gifts which are to be shared with love. You are unique and your way of sharing that gift may be different from the way another person might share.

Our life purpose lies within the way we share our gifts. There are many ways to teach, there are many ways to serve, there are many ways to give, to encourage, to lead and show mercy. Matthew 5:16 says, *"Let your light so shine before men, that they may see your good works and glorify your Father in heaven."*

We are here on this earth to help one another by using the gifts that God has bestowed upon us to glorify Him.

What are your gifts? How will you use your gifts?

DAY 64

DAY 65

But Never Give up

*"And let us not grow weary while doing good, for in due
season we shall reap if we do not lose heart."*

Galatians 6:9

To "lose heart" is like giving up. Why would you give up if what you are going through is temporary? Would you give up if you knew that God has a plan and good things in store for you in His time? As 2 Corinthians 4:17 says our affliction is *"but for a moment"* and *"is working for us a far more exceeding and external weight of glory."* Remember for God *"one day is as a thousand years, and a thousand years as one day"* (2 Peter 3:8). Our affliction may seem to last a long time, but not to Him.

Life is not easy and when we have our minds set on pursuing life goals, especially God's purpose for our life, unfortunately, attacks will come, and we get tired and want to give up. It is then that we should do all we can do to remain strong *"in the power of His might* (Ephesians 6:10)," through prayer and the reading of His Word so that we can endure whatever lies ahead.

There are times we might go down the wrong path, times we may make mistakes and wrong choices. It's important to learn from those mistakes and choices and bounce back. These are learning experiences and we must never give up. As I have said, when you begin to fulfill God's purpose for your life things will change for the better.

Salvation is the gift of God and not of works (Ephesians 2:8-9). As we do good (as much as we can) we will reap the blessings that God has in store for us (Galatians 6:9). Be encouraged!

What can you do now to keep moving forward and not give up?

DAY 65

DAY 66

Betrayal

*"Now as they were eating, He said, 'Assuredly, I
say to you, one of you will betray Me.' "*

Matthew 26:21

Even Jesus was betrayed. Judas Iscariot betrayed Him for thirty pieces of silver (Matthew 26:15). This disciple, someone who lived with Jesus, walked with Him, and talked with Him every day for three years. Depending on who your offender is, the closer the relationship, the deeper the betrayal.

Feelings of betrayal can be felt as it relates to the offender and non-offender who knew or should have known what was happening to you. Yes, the offenders may be living their lives as though nothing ever happened, but we don't know that for sure. There are some who may be remorseful and long to be forgiven. We may never know. What is important is that we find a way to get unstuck and move on with our lives.

It is not clear whether Jesus forgave Judas. However, while on the cross Jesus says in Luke 23:34, *"Father, forgive them, for they know not what they do."* This could have included Judas. So why should we not forgive? Remember, Jesus also says that we are to forgive others as He has forgiven us (Ephesians 4:32).

Who was your Judas?

Will you forgive them?

DAY 66

DAY 67

The Importance of Self-Compassion and Self-Love

"And you shall love the Lord your God with all your heart,
with all your soul, with all your mind, and with all your
strength. This is the first commandment. And the second,
like it, is this: 'You shall love your neighbor as yourself."

Mark 12:30-31

Self-love does not mean being conceited or narcissistic. It does not mean being self-absorbed or being selfish. How can we truly love others, which God commands us to do, if we do not love ourselves? It is not the earthly kind of love as we humans claim to express. It is a spiritual love, a divine love that can only come from God and His Spirit within us which works in us and through us.

Self-hatred is a sign of low self-esteem. Learning to love yourself is as important as your love for a close friend. Self-love is accepting yourself as you are, the good, the bad and the ugly and being kind towards yourself. Bring the real you to light! Be your own best friend!

Just as you would treat a close friend or beloved family member, it is important to treat yourself with compassion. You may not have been loved during your childhood, been abused, bullied, or called names. You may be in an intimate relationship where you are being physically, emotionally, and mentally abused resulting in self-loathing. You did not deserve what happened to you. You do not deserve what is happening to you now. How would you respond to a friend or family member who experienced what you have had to endure?

Can you think of some self-love activities to do to build your self-esteem? Write at least 10 **positive** things about yourself and recite them daily. Say to yourself "I'm alive, I survived, and I am learning how to thrive!"

DAY 67

I am _____

I am _____

I am _____

I am _____

I am _____

I am _____

I am _____

I am _____

I am _____

I am _____

_____

_____

_____

_____

_____

_____

_____

_____

_____

_____

_____

_____

_____

DAY 68

Know Yourself

"For what I am doing, I do not understand. For what I will
to do, that I do not practice; but what I hate, that I do."

Romans 7:15

As has been mentioned, you are not your trauma but because of unresolved trauma signs linger and you might not understand why you do what you do or say what you say that may be hurtful to others and yourself. It may be difficult for you to do in the moment what you know is right and instead you do what you hate. Only to regret it later. Give this some thought and search for an understanding of the reasons why. Are these actions, behaviors, thoughts, and feelings trauma-related? If you are unable to figure it out on your own, a professional can help you with that.

Know what triggers you for negative feelings and behaviors. Become aware of any negative self-talk and correct it. Determine if the things that you tell yourself are true. For example, can you handle criticism, if not why? Know if you are able to face life challenges. Know what makes you happy. Know what your dream job is and work towards obtaining it as a goal. Become aware of the accomplishments you are proud of and cherish them. Know what your hobbies are and engage in them on a regular basis.

What are your values? Do you have boundaries, or need to learn how to set boundaries?

What do you like about yourself? What do you dislike? What can you do to improve on the things you do not like about yourself?

What are your talents and skills? What do you do well? What are your favorite things, favorite songs?

DAY 68

DAY 69

Equip Yourself

*"Put on the whole armor of God, that you may be
able to stand against the wiles of the devil."*

Ephesians 6:11

Equipping yourself is preparing yourself to be emotionally, mentally and physically fit. This verse refers to equipping yourself to stand against evil and deception. Deception could have played a part in your becoming a victim at a time when you may have been the most vulnerable. Shame on those who used you and deceived you.

As a trauma survivor aiming to thrive, it is crucial for you to prepare yourself for what you might encounter each day. Try to identify people, places, things you might encounter each day that could possibly trigger a trauma response. Think about how you have responded in the past and how you could respond differently. Identify different ways of responding to those triggers and ways to cope with things that might cause you to become distressed.

Another suggestion for equipping yourself is to learn how to set boundaries and how you will defend those boundaries to protect yourself. If we allow others to treat us poorly, we could be leaving ourselves open to being retraumatized and open to continuing mistreatment.

Learn how to assert yourself which speaks again to reclaiming your voice. Know what you will accept and what you will not accept when setting boundaries in relationships.

Types of boundaries, to name a few, are physical, emotional, mental, time, and personal boundaries.

What boundaries have you set for each of these types of boundaries?

DAY 69

DAY 70

Healing for Your Inner Child
*"Behold, You desire truth in the inward parts, and in the
hidden part You will make me to know wisdom."*

Psalm 51:6

Who is your inner child? It is widely known that the concept of the inner child is attributed to psychiatrist Carl Jung. Early in childhood when negative experiences such as sexual, physical, emotional, and mental abuse occur, that injured child remains with us as we grow into adulthood. This is our inner child. The damage done has lasting effects well into adulthood, if not addressed. I call them invisible scars, the scars that others cannot see.

It's important to connect with your inner child to heal from the inside out. Acknowledging and reparenting that wounded child within you can be beneficial to your healing. Be empathetic towards the child-you, that little girl who may not have been loved as you can love her.

What happened to you back then was not your fault, it was something done to you as has been said many times. Think of a child who is the same age as you were when you were abused. Look at that child. Would you blame that child if it happened to her or him? I hope that you will do whatever you can to protect the children in your life from harm.

Look at a picture of yourself as a child. What were your unmet needs then?

What are your unmet needs now? How can those needs be met today?

Write a letter to your child-self. What can you do or say to make peace with your child within and make her feel loved? What can you say or do to help your inner child heal?

DAY 70

DAY 71

Prove Those Naysayers Wrong!

"When the wicked, even mine enemies and my foes, came
upon me to eat up my flesh, they stumbled and fell."

Psalm 27:2 (KJV)

There is a song by MercyMe called *"Greater."* In it they sing about hearing negative things about ourselves in our own minds and from the mouths of others, but how God sees us differently and what God says about us are good things.

There will be people who try to discourage you and judge you, and those who do not believe you can do what God has set before you to do. Often when we try to do good things that may seem impossible, we are faced with naysayers. Jealousy could be at play. It doesn't matter what they say. Ignore them or walk away and prove those naysayers wrong! As much as we might want them to believe in us, we don't need their approval. What matters is what God says and what He thinks. Right? They are entitled to their opinions, but you know what is said about opinions, everybody has one!

Is it possible you may even doubt yourself and learned that mindset by listening to the disparaging, belittling remarks from your parents, from your spouse, from other family members and so-called friends? Well, this can be unlearned. If you know in your heart that what you are doing is what you are supposed to do, are doing it to the best of your ability and it is lined up with God's purpose for your life, don't let anyone stop you! Again, I say, prove those naysayers wrong!

Do you feel the need to have the approval of others? Why?

Name a goal or something the Lord has set on your heart to do. Will you pursue it?

DAY 71

DAY 72

Hang in There!
"The end of a thing is better than its beginning; The patient in spirit is better than the proud in spirit."

Ecclesiastes 7:8

It may seem that the things you hope and pray for are a long time coming. Time passes quickly for God when even a day, sometimes for us, seems to go so slowly as we wait for answers to our prayers.

Patience is needed along this journey. Someone who needs your support, encouragement and wisdom is waiting for you! Stay in prayer as you go. Stay strong, be patient and persevere. I was well into my adulthood before I learned what God's purpose was for my life. Remember, God's desire is for us is to prosper and be in good health (3 John 1:2) and He will be with you wherever you go (Joshua 1:9). As He says in the scripture above, the ending is better than the beginning. Hopefully this refers to life. You can't give up!

There will be difficult lessons that need to be learned along the way. This is part of the growing process, especially after trauma. There will be hills and valleys, highs and lows but once you discover what your life purpose is and begin to walk in it, I believe your life will change for the better. You will find joy in that purpose.

Learn how to keep yourself motivated and surround yourself with positive, inspiring people.

List your reasons for not giving up.

What do you need to do to keep moving forward – next steps?

DAY 72

DAY 73

The Importance of Prayer
"Now this is the confidence we have in Him, that if we ask anything according to His will, He hears us."

1 John 5:14

Throughout this devotional, references are made to praying. There is power in prayer and 1 Thessalonians 5:17 says that we should *"pray without ceasing."* You may know, we can pray anywhere because God is with us wherever we go, and He hears us.

Faith and prayer go hand and hand. James 1:6 says when praying ask in faith without doubt. Prayer changes things but does that mean things will turn out the way we hope? Not always. God knows the desires of our hearts and He knows what is best for us.

Prayer brings us closer to God and strengthens our relationship with Him. Prayer is communication with Him. It's not just asking for this or that but talking to Him like you would a confidant. Prayer is pouring your heart out to Him knowing that He hears us and is listening to every word. It's letting Him know you are aware of His promises and are aware of what He expects of us.

He knows we will fall short from time to time, no one is perfect, and He knows our heart. He knows us better than we know ourselves. Although He knows all, He still wants to hear from us.

Answers from Him can be yes, no, wait.

Have you been praying and have not gotten any answers?

Will you continue to pray? If not, why not?

What if the answer is wait?

DAY 73

DAY 74

The "Littles"

"Train up a child in the way he should go and
when he is old he will not depart from it."

Proverbs 22:6

I once heard someone refer to their children as "the littles." It struck me as a term of endearment. I wish I had been more nurturing as a parent, but attempting to parent in a traumatized state, I did not know how and fell short. I was emotionally unavailable for my child. I did not recognize the signs of unresolved trauma that I was experiencing and did not know where to go for help. By the time I got the help I needed, my child had reached adulthood.

It's not too late for you! You must take care of you NOW, so that you can effectively parent, love and nurture *your* "littles" the way they need to be loved and nurtured. I failed at this and wish I knew then (while raising my child) what I know now. Yet, I am thankful for God's forgiveness, encouragement, strength, healing, and wisdom so that I have been able to help mothers who came after.

Some things you should know though is, as much as we love our children, they can unknowingly trigger traumatic memories of what happened to us in our past. This is especially true as it relates to childhood sexual abuse. When a child reaches the same age as you were when you were sexually abused, memories of what happened to you can be triggered. You may become overprotective, which is not necessarily a bad thing, fearing that your child could also be victimized.

Being aware of this is important to identifying triggers and recognizing the need to learn how to parent in a nurturing and healthy way as you seek help with resolving the trauma you have endured. It may not be too late for you to ensure you are properly caring for your "littles."

For information about how to protect your children from sexual abuse go to the Darkness to Light website at www.d2l.org.

DAY 74

DAY 75

Be Revived

"I will never forget Your precepts, For by them You have given me life."

Psalm 119:93

You may have heard of church revivals. I'm thinking revival is about renewing one's relationship with God, Jesus, and the Holy Spirit, and developing or renewing relationships with like-minded people. A time to be restored, re-energized, and revived. To come alive again.

Coming alive again, being restored after a traumatic event takes a desire to recover, time and hard work. Enduring and going through a traumatic experience is like losing your true self. It's a pivotal moment that changes *everything* and what happened to you can't be changed.

Trauma changes your view of self, others, and the world. The world may no longer be viewed as a safe place. Perhaps people who you once trusted can no longer be trusted. Your sense of self-worth, self-esteem and self-confidence are damaged, and shame, self-blame, and self-hatred come to the forefront. These responses to trauma are normal but should not remain. There comes a time to focus on your recovery, for you to be revived and made whole.

Revival can be the reviving of your true self; again, this takes time, it's a process and you may need professional help along the way to learn new ways of coping, different ways of responding, how to heal and learn to love yourself again. This verse (Psalm 119:93) says that God's teachings give life. Meditating on His Word can be helpful to the healing process. Identifying scripture that comforts, encourages, and speaks of healing has worked for me. Perhaps it will work for you.

What steps will you take towards being revived again and to begin to thrive?

Which scripture will you meditate on as part of your healing process?

DAY 75

DAY 76

Embrace Your Truth
"The Lord is near to all who call upon Him,
To all who call upon Him in truth."

Psalm 145:18

If you are the victim of childhood sexual abuse, neglect, rape or domestic violence, the odds may be against you when you share your truth. It's possible you may not be believed. It's possible people may think you are "crazy" and falsifying the story you tell. It hurts when you tell the truth and are not believed. God knows the truth, so hold on and embrace your truth.

Often with childhood sexual abuse the child is not believed which contributes to the damage already done. Why would a child lie about something like this?

Domestic violence is also often not believed. Should you seek help from the authorities you need proof. You may hear things like "he is such a nice guy and wouldn't do anything like that." But no one knows what goes on behind the closed doors of your home or your neighbor's home. Horrific things could be happening there too as you and I well know.

Being in denial and pretending that what happened to you has not negatively affected you can cause more harm mentally. Facing the truth can be frightening but necessary. Ignoring the signs of unresolved trauma will prevent you from getting the help that you need.

Embrace your truth! And as you do, with the Lord's help, you will be free of those chains that bind you. There is a song called *"Break Every Chain"* sung by Tasha Cobbs that speaks of the power of Jesus, enough to break those chains.

What could be the consequences of not getting the help that you need? "The Lord is near" and is waiting for you to call upon Him. Will you?

DAY 76

DAY 77

Your True Self

"For we are His workmanship, created in Christ Jesus for good works, which God prepared beforehand that we should walk in them."

Ephesians 2:10

Trauma changes a person. There is the loss of a sense of self and not knowing who you truly are. Trauma distorts your belief about self. Your true self is who God created you to be. God knew you before He formed you in your mother's womb as He says in Jeremiah 1:5 and had plans for you from the beginning.

Ask, and He will let you know what His plans are for your life and lead you back to your true self. You are unique; there is no one else like you. You are who you are by the grace of God as is said in 1 Corinthians 15:10. You are a work in progress and created for *"good works."* When you recognize that something is wrong with the way you feel, or the way you think, or the way you behave, know that you must do something about it and God has a plan for you.

Because of the abuse I suffered as a child, I didn't like people, I didn't trust people and kept my distance from others. I was shy, withdrawn and rarely spoke. But I knew this was not my true self. I had no way to escape the abuse, but I felt God was with me and helping me through it. I often asked Him why and not until I became an adult did I know the answer. He knew I was strong enough to withstand the abuse. He knew that His plan for me was to help women survivors who are in need of help, and He chose me to help them because of my own traumatic experiences and healing journey. My continued prayer was (and continues to be) that as a counselor God would send to me only those women who *He* knew I would be able to help. It has been a blessing and an honor to have been able to do just that.

Use three words to describe your true self. What is something fabulous about you? (Nothing is not an acceptable answer!)

DAY 77

DAY 78

Can You Hear Me?
"It shall come to pass that before they call, I will answer;
And while they are still speaking, I will hear."

Isaiah 65:24

When children say that they are being sexually abused they are often not believed. When a child is being bullied in school, it is often ignored. In some cases, children are afraid to tell, but there are other signs that something is not right which adults do not notice or pretend not to see. When a traumatized child acts out or their grades in school suddenly plummet it is quite often a cry for help, which can go unnoticed.

If you are being battered and abused in a domestic relationship, fear may prevent you from leaving and asking for help. Fear may even cause you to try to cover up what is happening. You may hope that people on the outside will *hear* with their eyes and step in to help.

When battered women gain the courage to report domestic violence, they are often told they need evidence that abuse is taking place. Those close may be aware of what is happening but may not know what to say or do. Hopefully, if you are currently living with an abusive spouse, you are working on a plan for safety.

The telling of any abuse can be scary and leaving an abusive relationship can be dangerous. As you read this devotional, if you are currently in a dangerous situation, you can either call 911, your local authorities or the National Domestic Violence Hotline 1-800- 799-SAFE (7233) which is available 24/7. They will listen and they will hear you. Those on the Domestic Violence Hotline should be able to assist you with developing a plan for safety and help you to safely leave, if that is what you choose to do. Should you decide to reach out for help, please do so in a safe manner.

And yes, God hears you when you call out to Him through prayer. You must sit still and listen for His answers. He will help and guide you.

DAY 78

DAY 79

Stepping Stones

"He also brought me up out of a horrible pit, Out of the miry clay, And set my feet upon a rock, And established my steps."

Psalm 40:2

God will bring you up out of that "horrible pit," if He has not done so already. It takes time. Be patient as you move forward on your pathway to healing taking one step at a time. God promises He will direct our steps (Proverbs 16:9) in His Word. Consult and meditate on His Word for guidance.

Stepping stones for climbing out of the miry clay and being healed from unresolved trauma could look something like this: being aware and acknowledging something is wrong; seeking help from a professional who specializes in trauma recovery; identifying your support system - those people who will remain by your side as you travel your pathway to healing; identifying your personal goals along the way and fulfilling those goals; not only forgiving others but also forgiving yourself; being willing to do whatever it takes to recover; meditating on the Word daily; and praying without ceasing for guidance and healing.

Recovery is not an easy process and progress may be slow and depends upon your level of commitment. Being willing to take one step at a time may be best. It takes dedication. There will be bumps along the way, but God will place your feet upon the Rock who is He, the foundation, shield, and stronghold (Psalm 18:2).

What will it take for you to be open to the possibility of being made whole and taking the steps necessary to make it happen?

DAY 79

DAY 80

Through the Darkest Valley

"When you pass through the waters, I will be with you; And through the rivers, they shall not overflow you. When you walk through the fire, you shall not be burned; Nor shall the flame scorch you."

Isaiah 43:2

God is with us wherever we go even in the darkest valley. There is a song by Lynda Randle called *"God on the Mountain."* It may not be your kind of music, just listen to the words! (Remember words are powerful!) She speaks of God being with us during the good times and bad, the ups and the downs. God does not change and remains who He says He is no matter the circumstance. He remains loyal to us, so we should remain faithful to Him. He promises He will never leave or forsake us and encourages us to not be afraid (Deuteronomy 31:6).

As I struggled during my childhood and early adulthood, I often stood at my bedroom window and prayed. I cried out to God and asked that He let me feel His presence and He did! A feeling would come over me that is difficult to explain but which felt reassuring to me and reminded me that I was not alone. Another time shortly after praying, as strange as this might sound, I felt a hand gently touch my shoulder when no one else was around which I took as a sign from God that everything was going to be okay.

When you read Isaiah 43:2 above, what does it bring up for you? Although you may be different because of what happened to you, you survived it. You were not alone; He was with you. Then why, you might ask, did He not intervene and save you during your darkest hours? We may never know the answers to these types of questions, but God promises that all things work together for good (Romans 8:28).

Is there a scripture verse you can meditate on to help you when you are experiencing a dark valley moment?

DAY 80

DAY 81

Remember Whose You Are

"But as many as received Him, to them He gave the right to become children of God, to those who believe in His name: who were born, not of blood, nor of the will of the flesh, nor of the will of man, but of God."

John 1:12-13

As Christians, the Holy Spirit of God lives within us. Jesus says He abides in us and we in Him (John 15:5). That means we are His. There is comfort in knowing that.

Think about this:

Because we are His, our sins are forgiven (1 John 1:9).

Because we are His we are loved (John 3:16).

Because we are His we are overcomers (1 John 4:4).

Because we are His we are "more than conquerors" (Romans 8:37).

Because we are His we have access to Divine guidance, the Holy Spirit, our Helper (John 14:26).

Because we are His we can be healed, and He redeems our life from destruction. (Psalm 103:3-4)

Because we are His we have a purpose for living (Ephesians 2:10).

Because we are His we are new creations and all things become new (2 Corinthians 5:17).

What is it that you believe about who you are?

Does it line up with what He says about whose you are? If not, why not?

DAY 81

DAY 82

Jesus Knows, Know Him

*"For if our heart condemns us, God is greater
than our heart, and knows all things."*

1 John 3:20

Jesus is our Savior and gateway to God. He knows all that you have been through. He knew you before you were born (Jeremiah 1:5). He knows your name and even the hairs on your head are numbered (Luke 12:7). He knows what you need before you ask (Matthew 6:8). He knows about the child abuse, the neglect, the domestic violence, and abandonment. He knows all things. Do you know Him?

God's love is love like no other and it's unconditional. He loves us just the way we are, although His desire is that we become what He created us to be so that we can fulfill His purpose through our lives. Do you yet know what your purpose is?

We can turn our backs on God, which often happens after trauma because we don't understand why He would allow horrific things to happen. But He will never turn His back on us. So, if you have drifted away from Him, I hope you will find a way to genuinely know Him and reconnect. When you draw near to Him, He will draw near to you (James 4:8). A way to know Him is to know what He says in His Word which will help you feel His love for you and make you aware of your need for Him.

If you are experiencing guilt, shame, self-blame and suffering from self-condemnation, you should know that *"God is greater than [your] heart"* according to 1 John 3:20 above. He says there is no condemnation for those who believe in Him (Romans 8:1; John 3:18).

How will you get to truly know Jesus?

DAY 82

DAY 83

He Came for You!
"The thief does not come except to steal, and to kill, and to destroy. I [Jesus] have come that they may have life, and that they may have it more abundantly."

John 10:10

Jesus loves you unconditionally. I've heard it said that Jesus loves each one of us as though we were the only one to love. If you were the only person on earth, He would have gone to the cross just for you! That's love!

Research has revealed that the word "thief" in this verse means one who steals. It is known that the devil (Satan) is a thief who steals, kills, and destroys. A 2016 Gallup poll shows that only 61% of Americans believe in the devil. Do you? Because of God's plan for our lives from the time we were in our mother's womb, the devil attempted to destroy us, we who are the called.

Fortunately, Jesus came so that we, His "sheep," would live and have abundant lives. He wants for us good things, but we have free will. With free will we sometimes do things we should not do and avoid things we should do. This is even more pronounced in those who are survivors of trauma. Remember the reference to Romans 7:15 which says we do not understand why we do the things we do and *"what I hate, that I do"*? These are the things that cause us to take a wrong turn and head down the wrong path.

Thank God for His Son, Jesus, through whom we receive love, grace, mercy and forgiveness which is motivation for us to get back on track and pursue that abundant life He desires for us.

Do you believe He came for you?

What path are you on? Is it the right path? If not, why not?

DAY 83

DAY 84

What is Your Pathway to Healing?
"Let your eyes look straight ahead, And your eyelids look right before you. Ponder the path of your feet, And let all your ways be established. Do not turn to the right or the left; Remove your foot from evil."

Proverbs 4:25-27

This is something you must figure out for yourself. Your pathway to healing is unique to you. Your journey is your journey. Your life purpose is unique to you. Pray about the steps you should take that lead to your pathway to healing and then walk in it. When you are on the right path you will begin to recognize what is the right thing to do and do that thing. You will also recognize and do what makes you happy. The people around you may not like the change they see in you. They are used to the old you, the grumpy you, the angry you, the sad you, the you who was filled with self-loathing. But those who truly love and care for you will rejoice with you.

The healing process is not easy and maybe even scary at times. I cannot stress this enough. There will be people, places, things that attempt to knock you off your pathway to healing. Hang in there and remember God is with you always and you can always call on Him. Those who love and care for you will remain with you, help guide you and will be available for support.

Also, as you start your journey, a therapist, counselor, or pastor who is trained and has experience working with trauma survivors should be able to help you along the way. Keep in mind it's your choice when and if you decide to share your story. If you decide to share, be sure it is with someone you trust, share only as much or as little as YOU would like and go at YOUR own pace.

What will be your first step on your pathway to healing?

DAY 84

DAY 85

Angels Along the Way
*"For He shall give His angels charge over
you, To keep you in all your ways."*

Psalm 91:11

Angels are sent by God. Each has an assignment, a mission to help whomever God sends them to for help. The Angels that I speak of here (sometimes ordinary people like you and me, sometimes people we know or could be strangers) may not be aware that what they are doing or saying was given to them by God to do or say. You may have unknowingly been an Angel along the way. It's a God thing! We were put here on this earth to help one another.

We encounter what I call Angels Along the Way, sometimes without realizing that God has placed that person in our life for a minute to deliver a word, an hour, a day, a week, or a year for the sole purpose of helping us through a difficult time. They may not know, and you may not know (at the time) that they are an Angel sent by God. You may recall stories of people being helped out of dangerous situations by strangers who seem to simply disappear and nowhere to be found after the danger has passed. Could they have been one of God's Angels Along the Way?

In my own life I can recall a time when my sister unexpectedly came to visit. At that very moment, my then fiancé was threatening my life when my sister walked in. Usually, the door to my home is locked but that day, for whatever reason, it was not, and she entered. She was able to talk that man down which literally saved my life. She was my Angel that day. I have no doubt she was sent there at just the right time by God. There are many other stories of Angels Along the Way I could tell.

Challenge yourself to identify the Angels you have experienced along the way. They could have been there for a reason or a season, for a minute or an hour. Who has been your Angel along the way?

DAY 85

DAY 86

You are Unique and That's a Good Thing

"But now, O Lord, You are our Father; We are the clay, and You our potter; And all we are the work of Your hand."

Isaiah 64:8

What would this world be like if we were all the same? Boring! God is so-o-o-o-o creative. We are all human beings, but He made us to look different, speak differently and be different on purpose. Each one of us is unique. And God's creations do not stop with us. Take another look at the birds in the sky, the fish in the sea, the animals that roam the earth, the stars, the sun, and the moon in the sky. Wow! Amazing!

Do you compare yourself to others and think of yourself as less than? Why? Do you not know you are unique, in a good way? God has a plan for you and made you the way you need to be to fulfill His purpose for your life and to His glory. Seek it, find it, and walk in it! Because you are unique, God has a unique purpose just for you.

Strive to be who He created you to be. In 1 Corinthians 15:10 it says, *"by the grace of God I am what I am."* All of us have our own individual assignment. I hope you will soon find the assignment that is meant for you and fulfill it despite past sufferings.

Your life may have been disrupted because of what has happened to you. What happened to you cannot be changed, but the automatic trauma responses can be done away with or managed and coping skills learned. You must do the work. Don't give up on yourself. God will never give up on you.

What are some talents and skills that make you stand out from the crowd?

DAY 86

DAY 87

Like a Palm Tree

"The righteous shall flourish like a palm tree, he shall grow like a cedar in Lebanon. Those who are planted in the house of the Lord shall flourish in the courts of our God. They shall still bear fruit in old age; they shall be fresh and flourishing . . ."

Psalm 92:12-14

You've been through a lot, through the storms of life, trials, and tribulations. Still YOU SURVIVED. You made it through and thus far you have been able to bear it.

Years ago, I heard a sermon about palm trees. The pastor spoke of how, with God's help, we can be resilient like a palm tree and bounce back. This pastor shared how a palm tree bends but won't break. Even when its branches are blown by the wind and bent to the ground it bounces back. (Another of God's great creations.)

Research indicates that some palm trees can grow up to 60 feet tall and can live to be over 100 years old, depending on the type. This Psalm states that *"the righteous shall flourish like a palm tree."* Flourish means to thrive which is the ultimate goal for a survivor of trauma.

For some, the palm tree symbolizes the "tree of life." In Revelation 22:2 it is said that the leaves of the "tree of life" were for the healing of nations.

When we are grounded and rooted in the Word of God, we can survive the storms, trauma, and trials of life which are meant to make us stronger. We can be flexible, bend and hopefully not break like the palm tree and bear fruit (remain useful and productive) even in our old age.

What can you do to stand strong like a palm tree?

DAY 87

DAY 88

Seek Wise Counsel

*"Where there is no counsel, the people fall; But in
the multitude of counselors there is safety."*

Proverbs 11:14

It is good to seek wise counsel who can suggest or advise. You may have a friend or a family member who you believe to be wise and who you can go to for advice. Friends and family with whom you feel safe can be a good source for advice on everyday issues but might not be knowledgeable about trauma-related issues.

If you are experiencing trauma-related issues, a trained professional may be what you need. It's an individual choice. Yes, there are many reasons people fear entering therapy. You can always at least try it and if it does not work you can always end it. It's worth a try for your mental wellbeing and safety.

If you decide to seek counseling, you must do your homework to find someone who meets your specific needs and suits you. During your search for a trained therapist, it is imperative to find someone who specializes and has experience in trauma recovery.

There are quite a few websites where you can search for a therapist who is trained to meet your specific needs. On these websites you can search for a Christian counselor, counselors by gender, specialty, type of therapy, type of insurance and more. (See the Resource list at the end of this devotional journal for the names of websites for finding a counselor.) It takes courage to reach out for this type of help. If you have the time, take the time to find the right counselor for you. Pray for the courage to reach out for help and for guidance in this regard.

Will you reach out?

What will your prayer be?

DAY 88

DAY 89

A Promise

"Behold, I will do a new thing,
Now it shall spring forth; Shall you not know it?"
I will even make a road in the wilderness
And rivers in the desert."

Isaiah 43:19

God has given us many promises. Too many to name here but just to name a few:

He promises an everlasting love (Jeremiah 31:3).

He promises to forgive us (1 John 1:9).

He promises never to leave us nor forsake us (Hebrews 13:5).

He promises to renew our strength (Isaiah 40:31).

He promises to supply all our needs (Philippians 4:19).

He promises to heal our wounds (Jeremiah 30:17).

He promises all things work together for good (Romans 8:28).

He promises He will strengthen us and help us (Isaiah 41:10).

He promises to complete a good work in us (Philippians 1:6).

Now, make a promise to yourself. Name one step you can take towards your healing. Make a promise to yourself that you will do it.

I promise to take at least this one step on my pathway to healing.

I will _____.

DAY 89

DAY 90

"Fly Butterfly, Fly"
*"Therefore, if anyone is in Christ, he is a new creation; old things
are passed away; behold, all things have become new."*

2 Corinthians 5:17

Remember the poem *Fly Butterfly, Fly* at the beginning of this devotional journal. It speaks of a caterpillar crawling and screaming for help, but no one hears. Also remember that through stages caterpillars turn into beautiful butterflies. We, as humans, also go through stages of development. Some of these stages are infancy, early childhood, early school years, adolescence, and adulthood. At any stage in our lives, we could, and for some have, experienced a traumatic event. But those things are now "passed away" and all things are becoming new. You can look forward to tomorrow as "the first day of the rest of your life" and do all you can do to make each day the best day of your life!

You can be okay and recover from the abuse you have suffered. Ask for the help you need. There is no shame in that. Jesus is waiting for you and says in Revelation 3:20, *"I stand at the door and knock."* Will you let Him in? GOD LOVES YOU!!! JESUS LOVE YOU!!!

*"For I am persuaded that neither death nor life, nor angels nor
principalities nor powers, nor things present nor things to come,
nor height nor depth, nor any other created thing, shall be able to
separate us from the love of God which is in Christ Jesus our Lord."*

Romans 8:38-39

Jesus set me free and placed my feet on solid ground. He did it for me, He will do it for you!

Who are the women you know who have overcome trauma and now thrive?

What will you do to go from being a caterpillar to a beautiful butterfly?

Go forth and be a blessing!! Start now!

DAY 90

HELPFUL RESOURCES

(If you are in danger at any time or need emergency assistance, please call 911 or your local authorities immediately.)

National Suicide Prevention Lifeline: 1-800-273-TALK (8255) - This Lifeline provides 24/7, free and confidential support for people in distress; prevention and crisis resources for you or loved ones; website is www.suicidepreventionlifeline.org. The National Suicide Prevention Lifeline number in Spanish is 1-888-628-9454.

National Organization for Victim Assistance, at www.trynova.org, helps advocate for victims and connect victims to services and resources; and promotes public policy initiatives that protect the rights of crime victims and serves as the national voice.

Rape, Abuse and Incest National Network (RAINN), www.rainn.org – RAINN is the nation's largest anti-sexual assault organization and operates the National Sexual Assault Hotline at 1-800-656-HOPE (4673). It has programs to help victims and is instrumental with bringing rapists to justice.

Gift From Within – At www.giftfromwithin.org you will find more information and resources then you could even imagine. It is a non-profit organization whose focus is to help trauma survivors, those suffering from posttraumatic stress disorder and those who care about and care for trauma survivors. Here you will find educational material, videos, articles, books and other resources.

National Domestic Violence Hotline 1-800- 799-SAFE (7233); www.the-hotline.org- is available 24/7 to talk confidentially with anyone experiencing domestic violence, seeking help or information; this hotline is an immediate link to help for victims. It provides information and assistance to adult and youth victims of family violence, domestic violence, or dating violence, family and household members, and the general public. This website also provides a guide for creating a safety plan.

Warmlines – are peer-run listening lines, also called peer support lines, which are staffed by people in mental health recovery (not by mental health professionals); good for when you need someone to talk to but you are **not in crisis**; www.warmline.org lists warmlines by state.

Psychology Today – At www.psychologytoday.com you can search for a trauma therapist by location, by gender, by issue, insurance, type of therapy, according to your age and more.

Mental Health Match – At www.mentalhealthmatch.com you can easily find a trauma therapist that meets your needs with their free matching tool you can find a trauma therapist in your area by issue, gender, insurance, type of therapy and more.

Substance Abuse and Mental Health Services Administration (SAMHSA) National Helpline – 1-800-662-HELP (4357) is a confidential, free, 24/7, treatment referral and information service, available in English and Spanish and provides referrals to local treatment facilities, support groups, and community-based organizations for individuals and families facing mental and/or substance use disorders; www.samhsa.gov/find-treatment.

The National Parent Helpline – 1-855-427-2736; www.nationalparenthelpline.org; is a 24-hour crisis hotline for parents and caregivers and offers emotional support, helps problem solve and helps you connect with local services, among other things.

Darkness to Light – www.d2l.org – National Helpline: 866-FOR-LIGHT - Darkness to Light is a non-profit committed to empowering adults to prevent child sexual abuse. Their mission is to empower adults to prevent, recognize, and react responsibly to child sexual abuse through awareness, education, and stigma reduction for a world free of child sexual abuse.

The U.S. Department of Health and Human Services' Office on Women's Health – www.womenshealth.gov – Helpline: 1-800-994-9662. Their mission is to "improve the health of women and girls through policy, education, and innovative programs." There is a wealth of information about relationships and safety on this website.

***Because changes do occur, it is highly recommended that the phone numbers and websites for the resources listed above be verified **before** a need arises.*